T0244563

BOY WANTED

ON SAVILE ROW

BOY WANTED

ON SAVILE ROW

FROM APPRENTICE TO TAILORING ICON

A MEMOIR BY
TIMOTHY EVEREST MBE

The
History
Press

First published 2024

The History Press
97 St George's Place, Cheltenham,
Gloucestershire, GL50 3QB
www.thehistorypress.co.uk

© Timothy Everest, 2024

The right of Timothy Everest to be identified as the Author
of this work has been asserted in accordance with the
Copyright, Designs and Patents Act 1988.

All rights reserved. No part of this book may be reprinted
or reproduced or utilised in any form or by any electronic,
mechanical or other means, now known or hereafter invented,
including photocopying and recording, or in any information
storage or retrieval system, without the permission in writing
from the Publishers.

British Library Cataloguing in Publication Data.
A catalogue record for this book is available from the British Library.

ISBN 978 1 80399 389 8

Typesetting and origination by The History Press
Printed and bound in Great Britain by TJ Books Limited, Padstow, Cornwall.

Trees for Life

For my wife Catherine and
my daughters Carina and Alyssia.

I'd like to thank everybody who has worked for us
because without them there would be no me.

Timothy Everest

Contents

1

The Apex

The apex is the point at which you are closest to the inside of the corner, also referred to as the clipping point. Once you have hit the apex, you should be able to start increasing the throttle.

It's very common for drivers to apex too early. The racing line apex is often out of view at the point of turn in or further round the corner than you expect.

Every Thursday, a tailor used to set up a stall at Canterbury Market and for £5 you could commission a pair of trousers to your exact build and fit. As I think back to the genesis of my burgeoning fascination with clothes, my Thursday jaunts to Canterbury were what they refer to in astrophysics as the singularity – a context within which a small change can cause a large effect. I was obsessed with trousers. At that time, high-waisted trousers, three-button jackets with patch pockets on the side, platform shoes and tank tops were all the rage.

I used to wear those high-waisted trousers – all the way up to my armpits. The rise was accentuated even further because of the platform shoes, my very long legs and disproportionately small torso. This earned me the nickname 'Mini BOD', which my father would call me whenever I walked into the room.

Fashion, along with the music scene, would move very fast. You could follow the looks of the day through the prism of the music. My taste in clothes was always informed by the music movements and what people would be wearing to the clubs. And the late 1970s were a great time for music. You had disco (the Bee Gees, Michael Jackson), you had punk rock (the Clash, the Stranglers), and electronica was really taking off (Kraftwerk, Tangerine Dream). Part of going out was always dressing up and being able to put your look together. You had to be a chameleon. One night you might be wearing ripped Levi's and studded jean jackets snarling 'God Save the Queen'; the next, you're wearing sequined jumpsuits and thrusting your hips to 'Night Fever'.

I was living in Kent at the time, and with my education already going down the plughole, my parents had reluctantly resigned themselves to the fact I was going to be a dropout. Fashion and music aside, the only other thing that captured my attention growing up was the world of motorsports. Fundamentally, I had huge aspirations to be a racing driver.

A couple of my close friends and I saved up enough money and each bought the same silver CB 250N Honda Super Dream; the reason being, in a Honda Super Dream one could go from a 50cc to a 250cc straight away without having to take your driver's test – thus, enabling the driver to go from 40–50mph to 100mph, which resulted in many unfortunate deaths.

Mine was a TKT 314T. Our model numbers were sequential. My friends' were 312, 313 and I was 314. We roared around with reckless abandon, tearing through the local parishes and pockets of small villages that encircled Kent, trying desperately to reach the magical 100mph down the Thanet Way. Always in vain, however, as Super Dreams would max out at 96mph.

Racing around like lunatics with my friends merited me a sense of freedom. I took great pride in my Super Dream and meticulously cared for its upkeep. As I sped (quite literally) through the barriers of adolescence into adulthood I developed an enormous sense of independence.

However, my burgeoning career as a juvenile delinquent was drastically truncated when my mother, bless her, gave me two weeks to get a job – or else. I went to work in a shop called Lenleys, a deconstructed department store composed of little shops scattered around the butter market outside Canterbury Cathedral. Lenleys were suppliers of fine furniture and soft furnishings. There was a gay couple that used to run the soft furnishings department and there was more innuendo dished out by these two filthy minds in a morning's work, than in an entire series of *Are You Being Served?*

It was hilarious and I loved every minute of it.

The fun was soon curtailed as my parents decided it was time to move to Wales and start a new life running a restaurant. My grandfather, who was an underwater demolition expert, helped facilitate the move by transporting my Super Dream in the back of his van, along with all my other hopes and aspirations. Part of the deal of my parents buying the restaurant was securing a job for me as junior sales assistant in a company called Barretts, in Portfield, near Haverfordwest.

Six months later, it was an early summer's day and I was out on my Super Dream, ripping down a country lane and speeding in my usual feckless manner when disaster struck. A local teacher in a quite beautiful gold Ford Granada was overtaking an Electricity Board van around an apex where all the grass had grown high.

What happened next was a blur of swerving, tyres screaming, and the horrible 'GUTHUNK!' noise that can only be made with the sharp impact of large metal hitting large metal at high velocity. The obligatory somersaults ensued as I was catapulted into the long grass, rolling ungracefully before coming to rest a foot from a lamppost. My Super Dream was in bits, its metallic guts splayed across the asphalt like one of those disembowelled badgers you'd see that had fallen victim to roadkill. The teacher's car was also written off, I'd later learn, but assumed as much at the time. My knee suffered severe lacerations, and it must have looked pretty grim because when my mother arrived at the crash site, she took one look at it and burst into tears.

At the hospital they stitched me up. It needed fifty-two stitches in all. During the following months my spirits were high but my movements were quite restricted, to put it mildly. My knee and ankle locked up so badly it was as if the ligaments and thin tissue that binds the two had signed a secret treaty that an irreparable, implacable position would be for the greater good. To this day, I still have problems with my foot, but I've always considered myself fortunate to limp away from a crash of that magnitude. I've had friends who also believed themselves indestructible come off second best in those kind of situations with amputations or worse.

While I was busy doing very little but convalescing, I got a message through from my Great-Uncle Douglas that they were looking for a sales assistant in Hepworth's. Hepworth's was a thriving national chain of men's ready-made and made-to-measure suits based in Leeds. Back in those days, if you were looking to purchase your first suit, Hepworth's was one of the first places you would think to shop. Alongside the Fifty Shillings Tailor and Burton Menswear, Hepworth's ruled the roost as far as accessibly priced men's clothing was concerned for close to a century. They were beginning to reach the end of their rule, however, when I joined the business, and were to be absorbed entirely by Next plc by 1985.

Initially I thought it would be a bit boring. Tailoring in an old man shop? I'm not really into that.

'They'll pay you about £2.50 more a week than in your other job at Barretts,' my great-uncle said.

'That's quite good,' I replied, itching my ankle down the thin aperture of my ankle cast with a sewing needle. 'That'll buy me a lot of petrol for my new motorbike.'

'Fine, just don't repeat that crap to your mum. She's scared you'll end up like your Uncle Andy.'

My Uncle Andy had suffered a terrible motorcycle accident on the Guildford bypass twenty years before, breaking nearly every bone in his body. My grandmother was given the arduous and thankless responsibility of returning him back to Wales and nurturing his broken body back to health over the course of eighteen months.

Unfortunately for my dear grandmother's ticker, Uncle Andy had the racing bug. Once he was back on his brittle feet, he went straight down to the racing track in his souped-up Angular, nicknamed the 'Jangular' (a hybrid of the Jaguar Angular). The Jangular was a 1100cc with a straight-six E-type brace engine. The only drawback was it lacked the torque and dexterity to manoeuvre efficiently, if at all, around corners. Uncle Andy would often be seen careering off the track at 100mph when attempting to apex the corner at a complete opposite lock.

His death wish was not exclusive to car racing. In 1973, Uncle Andy saw the film *Live and Let Die* and was profoundly influenced by the scene where James Bond escapes Kananga's crocodile farm on a Glastron speedboat and is subsequently chased by Kananga's henchmen through the watery plains of Louisiana. This proved to be a trans-formative encounter in his evolution of thrill-seeking adventures and, together with his mate Rob, he bought the same Glastron speedboat days after watching the film.

He would hitch the Glastron to his Plymouth Barracuda, which he sprayed white with purple pinstripes to match the colour scheme of the boat, and with me and his girlfriend in the backseat, we'd tour the west coast of Wales, the soundtrack to *Shaft* blaring out of his eight-track stereo.

Once that novelty subsided, he got into racing karts. Initially, Uncle Andy showed some reluctance because racing karts had the reputation of being something kids would be forced to do before they were old enough to race proper cars. While that has some semblance of truth even today, karting is one of the purest and most economical forms of racing. With karting, you get to race four times. Three of those will be rounds of heats, which will ascertain where you start on the grid for the final race. This extra time on the track allowed drivers to hone their craft, learn about understeer, oversteer and become one with the kart. When Uncle Andy upgraded to a better one, I bought his first kart from him. And once again, just like I had been when I first drove my Super Dream, I was hooked.

We raced both the long and short circuits of Donnington at breakneck speeds. Our lap times were so fast that we defeated even those set by racers on the Moto GP bikes. Sure, they could outsprint us down the straights, but we were quicker around the corners. As my Uncle Andy would say, we went like 'shit off a shovel'. It was a great time, not only was I doing what I loved but it got me out of the doldrum of Wales as I travelled the country racing on different tracks.

With my newfound racing family we also lived fast off the track. Routinely, we'd spend all night out on the ale, returning to the track the next day with mind-crumbling hangovers and wondering why we struggled to get into the top ten, having qualified one and two on the grid the day before.

* * *

Back at the day job, I was finding my work at Hepworth's interesting, but not in the least bit fulfilling. Selling clothes was the antithesis of all the excitement and exhilaration that I lusted for at the tracks or in the clubs. However, when the managing director of the company, Alex Perry, visited the shop and, in no uncertain terms, earmarked me as the future of the business, I felt a sudden rush of belonging. Even if it was to a job that I was ambivalent towards. They dispatched me to training courses up and down the country. Gradually, as I became familiar with the structure of the business, the modicum of structure the work lent me in my own life became a welcome incursion.

A month later, I was offered the job of relief manager, an unfortunate title that could be easily misconstrued if one was of an immature mind. The true definition of a relief manager in the world of retail meant that if any of the store managers in south-west Wales fell ill or were otherwise indisposed, I would have to go and step in.

In a turn of good fortune, my Saturday boy in the Carmarthen store turned out to be an RAC marshal. An RAC marshal grants RAC licences to novices, measured on the number of races and hours one spends on the track. I called him my Saturday boy – ironically, he was a man in his mid-sixties, retired, quiet and very withdrawn at work. However, if you ever saw Saturday Boy at the racetrack, he would transform into a little Hitler. A horrible sadist who was drunk with power, disqualifying drivers on tedious technicalities and forcing them to race and prostitute their talents until they met his inscrutable standards. Luckily, Saturday Boy was not so scrupulous with me, and thanks to him, I got my racing licence fast-tracked, much to the bemusement of my Uncle Andy.

The training courses in Leeds taught me many aspects of the rag trade. How to sew, how to sell, and most importantly, how to listen. Our listening course had two very charming tutors. One was a big, hairy bear of a man and the other was a diminutive Jewish guy with the most slick-perfect combover I'd ever seen. Naturally, my attention was strained as I was more preoccupied with what club I'd be going to that night and what I'd be wearing, as opposed to listening to my tutors.

'You're not listening to us, are you, Timothy?' the tutors harmonised.

'Of course I am!' I blasted in quick defiance, with an eye-popping panic, as I was jolted back from future dancefloors into the sober orbit of the classroom.

'Perhaps you'd care to tell us your thoughts on *the* matter,' prompted the Bear.

A rush of blood swarmed over my cheeks and the synchronicity of head swivels and inquisitive eyes from my fellow classmates expunged small trickling beads of sweat from my temples. 'Sorry,' I folded with a sigh. 'You're right, I was distracted. I was thinking about the dancehall I was going to tonight, and what look I would put together.'

'And where are you going, might I ask?' asked Combover.

'The new cocktail bar down the city centre. The name escapes me, but I can find out for you.'

'Great,' the Bear interjected, with genuine interest. 'We'll see you there at 6 p.m. For now, if you wouldn't mind giving us the courtesy of your full attention, at least for the next twenty minutes.'

Later that evening, at 6 p.m. on the dot, I arrived at the Merrion Centre, our agreed rendezvous point. Bear and Combover were already in the bar, bookending two beautiful ladies who were laughing louder than their bright lemon pencil skirts. My presence at the bar brought an abrupt halt to the laughter. 'Timothy, you made it!' Combover exclaimed, placing his bottle of Red Stripe carefully on the bar behind him. Bear shook my hand and wrapped his arm around my shoulder. 'Ladies, this is Timothy, the young man I was telling you about,' Bear beamed, and the ladies smiled forcibly in tandem.

'Timothy's best asset, aside from his boyish good looks, is his listening skills,' Bear said. Combover nodded in agreement, introduced the ladies, then he and Bear excused themselves without explanation. Their bottles were only half-empty, so I assumed they would return. But as I stuttered and fumbled my way through the initial exchanges with the ladies, I realised why this meeting felt so contrived. Bear and Combover had left.

I ordered rounds of dirty martinis, to relax myself more than anything and decided to let the girls do the talking. After all, Bear and Combover had just billed me as the great listener, not a talker. I listened to them talk about their boyfriend troubles for the next three hours, which was quite easy as I'm fascinated with relationship troubles, unless it spirals into idle gossip.

The key thing I learnt that night was that sometimes people will talk to you about their problems ad nauseum and, just by externalising them, will work out the solutions themselves. The girls didn't need any advice from me – thankfully, as I had none to offer anyway.

It was quite the leap from talking to adolescent girls about wanting to be a racing driver to talking to grown-up women about their problems and issues. Turns out being a good listener is a life skill you can apply not just to woo girls, but in all walks of life. It was a skill I learned to hone very early on, and I still maintain it's one of the most important skills of being a good salesman. But we'll get on to that later.

As well as the listening courses, Leeds also served as a great station to set up base and hit the clubs on the weekend. My friends would also come up and we'd all hit Peter Stringfellow's club, Cinderella's. Or 'Cinders', as it was known to the locals. Next door was a 21 and over club called Rockerfella's. You had Cinders on one half, which was commercial, composed of girls bopping around their handbags and guys lassoing their ties around their heads having seen *Saturday Night Fever* one too many times, and the other half, Rockerfella's, was a little more exclusive and a lot more upmarket.

The exotic waitresses, seemingly poured into their bunny girl outfits, served as enough of a lure for footballers and celebrities alike. The rumour was that to keep punters there until the very end of the night, Peter Stringfellow always gave a bottle of bubbly away to any girl who would agree to getting naked on stage around closing time.

As I was only 18 at the time, the thrill of the night was always trying to sneak into the Rockerfella's section without being spotted by the bouncers. I managed to slip in once through an unmanned interconnecting door and revelled in decadence for all of five minutes before being identified by a scrupulous bouncer and being chucked out.

Back in Tenby, I had also befriended some like-minded individuals who pursued the enjoyment of fashion and music with equal verve. We'd hang around and DJ in a club called Crackwell. We would follow the trends through magazines like *The Face*, closely monitoring new bands, new sounds and new styles.

During the summer, we'd not only have friends that would come down from Kent, Manchester, Birmingham and other places, but we met other kids on holiday who were really pissed off because their parents couldn't afford to go to Spain, Italy or France. They had to go to bloody Tenby, of all places.

It was an odd coagulation of disparate youth, pushing promiscuously against the limitations of the beautiful but limited harbour town of Tenby. Constantly and vociferously seeking out the best clubs, the best after-parties. One night, after all the clubs shut, my best friend Stephen and his two brothers hotfooted it down to Narberth, having gotten wind of a big house party happening at a wealthy farmer's house.

As we pulled up to this huge Georgian building, seemingly unmoored from the rest of the houses in this small market town, I could hear the muffled thud of ELO's 'Showdown' emanating from the back of the house. The disco lights embroidered the canopies of the surrounding oak trees. As we sauntered around, we were greeted by a banquet of refinement. There was a big marquee furnished with several bars populated by well-heeled but now intoxicated middle-aged farmers and their wives and, more importantly, their daughters. Beyond the marquee stood a long swimming pool that finished at one end with water cascading down neon-lit steps.

We congratulated ourselves on our discovery. Anything to keep the night alive and at someone else's expense.

'This is so cool,' I beamed.

'So cool!' echoed Stephen. 'And you look cool, Tim.'

'Do I?' I said bashfully.

'Doesn't he look cool?' Stephen pointed to his brothers.

Collectively, they studied me up and down. I was wearing an oversized lemon tank top over an equally oversized white t-shirt and my cobalt blue pleated trousers were tapered down to my white Oxford canvas shoes. Continuously, I swept my peroxide blonde hair to one side with repeated strokes of my hand but had left my fringe to do its own thing.

'Too cool,' they agreed, almost in unison, eyeing the close proximity of the swimming pool.

Twigging the undercurrent of their compliments, I cautiously stepped back two paces to the lip of the swimming pool. With nowhere to go, they each grabbed a limb and with little grace tossed me into the pool, like a wooden crate onto a bonfire.

It was a great night, despite dripping my way through it. We caught the attention of a group of Brummies, whose parents also fell into the bracket of holidaying in Tenby because Spain was too rich for their blood. One of the guys, who we affectionately named Horse due to his massive overbite, informed us of this great club in Birmingham called the Rum Runner and that if we ever came to Birmingham, we should check it out.

Sure enough, accepting Horse's kind invitation (although he never remembered inviting us to crash on his floor), the following weekend we set off for Birmingham. I chose the New Romantic theme, with my pedal pushers, pumps and socks and a tartan sash over my shoulder. Simon Le Bon was there, and I later learned that the Rum Runner was owned by a guy who eventually went on to manage Duran Duran. Simon and I clocked each other, acknowledging and appreciating the fact we both had exactly the same crimped fringe and peroxide-blonde haircut. Although I sensed I was considerably more elevated by that than him.

It was the briefest of nods but one that gave me a sufficient boost. Things were starting to happen for me. Here I was mirroring the same set of looks as Simon Le Bon, and he looked cool. Ergo, I must look cool. Before I was always on the outside looking in, a voyeur and a student of the club scene and the stars that studded that world. For that briefest of moments, I was now on the other side of the rope, and I was being pulled willingly and without compromise, into that ecosphere.

We were like a band in a way, touring the clubs around the country every weekend with our crazy hair and our out-there looks. It was only a matter of time before we hit London.

2

Boy Wanted

Performing the doughnut manoeuvre can be extremely hazardous. Strain is placed on the vehicle's suspension and drivetrain, which may result in a mechanical breakdown with loss of control. In case of an emergency, you should always have people on standby.

Steve Strange started out doing artwork for Malcolm McLaren and the Sex Pistols, after being invited to London by Billy Idol. In the late seventies, he co-founded the Blitz Club, which gave birth to the Blitz Kids, who later morphed into the New Romantics. It was the perfect cocktail of music, fashion and glamour. Spandau Ballet played their first gigs there, and people were largely copying the Bowie look as he had just released 'Ashes to Ashes', the video of which was the most expensive ever made at the time and featured Steve Strange himself.

We forged our own set of looks, albeit heavily influenced by any given movement in music at the time. Fortunately, I was naturally curious about how fashion was intersecting with the club scene. Outside of what one might have gleaned from watching *Top of the Pops* every Thursday night or reading *Face Magazine*, the only way to absorb and garner inspiration for looks was by going to the clubs. There was no Internet, so no MR PORTER articles. You could buy elements of the looks on the High Street, Kensington, or the Great Gear Market on Kings Road, but you had to have the eye for it and curate your looks on your own. Those who didn't work on their own looks or didn't know how to put the looks together, those were the outsiders.

With each club having a different theme, one couldn't survive on just one set of looks. The same disco ensemble that I'd put together for Dodo's (which was a gay club) wouldn't cut it at a psychobilly-themed club.

By the late seventies, the angst of punk rock had punched itself out, to some degree. Electronica, although in its infancy, was generally apolitical and didn't necessarily have an identity with regard to looks anyway – that was, until rave came along. The New Romantic movement, spearheaded by the likes of Culture Club and The Cure, was still rife through the club scene. It had endured and absorbed some of the punk rockers who had wanted to jump ship.

Privately, I found the hot pursuit of dressing up, chasing girls and frightening them with make-up soon put an end to rebuilding the bottom end of a two-stroke engine on a Friday night. And every other night.

The Embassy Club on Bond Street was wall-to-wall celebrity, but you could get in if you knew the right people, preferably good-looking and reasonably well dressed. Also, in London at that time you had Camden Palace (now KOKO) plus Le Beat Route and White Trash. All of these clubs required different kinds of looks. It was a bit of a tightrope because you wanted to fit in to get in. But once you got in, you wanted to stand out.

When it came to putting our various looks together, we sourced the bulk of our clothes from a shop called Flip in Long Acre, Covent Garden. The theme of Flip was all-American clothing, conceived by a gentleman called Paul Wolf, who bought up loads of second-hand cheap jeans, baseball jackets, garish tuxedos and 1950s fleck sports jackets and shipped them to England. He had three stores in London, but we only went to the one on Long Acre. It was spacious but crammed with rows and rows of clothing. They set up shop in one those old fish market offices, so it didn't have to do much to attract the flea-market crowd.

No night – and no look – was ever the same, but no matter the theme, we knew we could go to Flip and find something to work with. If it was a Psychobilly night, we blow-dried our hair right up, bought big-printed shirts, cut the sleeves off, rolled them up and paired that with workwear jeans.

For the New Romantic nights, we had our hair down, tucked under a little cap, à la Steve Strange. I procured a beautiful, oversized evening shirt that I dyed cerise pink. Often, I'd pair that with some high-waisted cashmere stripes that could have been tailored originally for a wedding. All finished with spats shoes and a neckerchief.

One night, we ventured down to the Star Bar in Camden Palace. You couldn't miss me as I went dressed up as a white Rastafarian with white dreadlocks and a huge hat. Boy George came over and chatted me up. He was good fun and paid for all the drinks.

*   *   *

After a while, I caved to the wave of peer pressure and decided it was time to move to London. There were three of us who took the leap of faith: Stephen, who managed to get a job in a hair salon where my sister was working at the time, and Robert from the kitchen department in Hepworth's. He managed to get transferred and has been in the kitchen industry for over forty years. And then there was me.

I responded semi-begrudgingly to an advert in the *Evening Standard* for an operator at a call centre in Clapham. One cold Monday morning, I shuffled myself drearily off the train, over the concourse and ventured towards the anonymous-looking building tucked away behind the back of the station. My insides were churning. A compost of panic and uncertainty. Did I even want the job? Well, clearly not, but moreover, did I really want to put myself through the emotional upheaval of moving to London?

My interview was successful and whether I wanted it or not, the job was mine. Unsurprisingly, it was a deeply hollowing, insufferable experience. In just one day, I stole a quick glimpse into the bleak, interminable abyss that was my future as an operator in that call centre. It was a cold, ruinous landfill of broken dreams – what physicists would describe as an event horizon, where not even light could escape.

It was cauterised, however, by the flourish of unreal excitement I got by merely being in London itself. It felt like the centre of the earth, and the words of Jack Smith, 'Wilderness starts ten miles from the centre of London in any direction', truly resonated. I quit that job but continued vigorously to try to find something else that would plant me back there.

While mining the job section in the *Evening Standard*, two vacancies caught my eye. The first was for a salesman needed at Bonsack's Bonded Baths on Mount St. It was a very swanky shop that sold eclectic bathrooms and luxurious fittings, predominately in a period style, to the likes of hotels like Claridge's and tenants of traditional London townhouses and apartments.

I applied, writing a nice letter saying how I had a welter of experience in selling brass ornaments. I thought taps would be similar, but they thought otherwise. They replied with a beautiful handwritten letter wishing me luck, but rejected my application on the grounds that it would be far too traumatic for a young man to move to London, crystallising my own thoughts and pre-empting my anxieties.

The other advert had a headline that said, 'Boy Wanted on Savile Row'. Above the contact information read the name Tommy Nutter. As I did for Bonsack's Bonded Baths, I wrote a letter to Tommy Nutter applying for the post of the boy wanted. I didn't hear anything back.

Mike, my immediate boss at Hepworth's, took immense satisfaction in the absence of any reply. He just wanted to provoke me, and at any given opportunity would inform me that my prospects of getting a job at Tommy Nutter would be laughable. The more he teased me the more I'd summon the courage to go to the phone box on the corner at the end of the street, stick in my 2p and call Tommy. Every time I called, I was rebuked with either 'Oh Mr Nutter is very busy' or 'Mr Nutter is in a meeting' or 'No, Mr Nutter is in Brighton and couldn't possibly speak to you'.

Eventually, after the constant badgering they relented, and I managed to get an appointment with Tommy. I marched up to London wearing my oversized cobalt-blue double-breasted suit made at Hepworth's, manipulated from the made-to-measure block. Block colour was becoming very popular, and I had a broad range of block-coloured jackets made of lemon yellow, cerise and orange, all made one size or two sizes too big but very tight in the hip and paired with the obligatory high-rise trousers with pleats. My boss would agonise over my ensemble, 'Why the hell do you want that?' he bleated. 'They look so old-fashioned!' The irony of being lectured in style anachronisms from a man wearing a three-piece suit with flares in the year 1982 was not lost on me.

There were very few resources pre-Internet from which you could glean information about your potential employer. Safe to say, I knew nothing about Tommy Nutter before I met him at his tailoring house on Savile Row. I thought, 'Savile Row? Tailoring? Boring.' My ambition was to use this job as a conduit. Get a job on Savile Row, which would dovetail nicely into a job in fashion.

Tommy's PA was a lady named Catherine, who I thought was very posh. I waited with her while we waited for Tommy. My eyes shifted around nervously. The shop had been owned and furbished previously by a very famous retailer called John Michael. The smoked-glass windows had echoes of the Savile Row of yesteryear. The point being the tailors didn't want their customers peering in and seeing them at work. Ironically, it was Tommy Nutter and his cutting partner Edward Sexton who were the first to do away with those smoked-glass windows when they first launched House of Nutter on Savile Row in the late 1960s. Passers-by could see for the first time in full glory, beyond the window display of course, a Savile Row showroom.

I twitched my feet on the shagpile carpet and clocked the array of chrome fixtures that furnished the walls. It screamed 1970s. It screamed glamour. Sure, it would look terrific today as a shop-fit in a quasi-retro nostalgic way, but back then it was too on the nose and totally out of sync with what was going on at the time.

Tommy walked in wearing a sandy light tan double-breasted, three-piece flannel suit with a lovely burnt orange overcheck and little hints of blue. The shoulders were big, and it was slim through the hips – the archetypal Tommy Nutter silhouette that the whole world and I would later recognise. He had very baggy trousers finished with two-tone Maccabee shoes which I later bought off him because they were too big for him (I've still got them). He was in his late thirties but with the kind of cherubic features that could lead to a life of mischief. His hair was short and one length, modelled on the one Harrison Ford had during that time, which was simply referred to as the 'no haircut'.

He was handsome but more strikingly, Tommy Nutter was very, very cool. Where was the crusty old guy with bifocal glasses in a pinstripe suit peppered with dandruff that I was expecting?

'Do you know anything about me?' Tommy asked bluntly, sitting across from me and folding his arms. I could sense immediately he was indifferent to my choice of attire.

'Of course,' I lied. 'I know quite a bit about you.' I fidgeted and didn't elucidate any further.

'You don't know a thing about me,' he quickly surmised.

'You're right, I don't. Sorry,' I blushed.

'Catherine, can you get the press folders.'

Catherine dutifully disappeared and returned with several folders, all with cloth-covered jackets 3in thick. He slid them across the table like they were yesterday's newspapers.

I was aghast when I turned to the first page and saw cuttings of The Beatles in full Tommy Nutter regalia.

'Oh my god!' I said, genuinely astonished. 'The Beatles, what did you do with them?'

'Oh, I dressed them,' Tommy said casually. 'Not in this store. I used to have another studio just down the Row. That's where I'd hang out with them.'

I turned the page and saw a cutting of the famous *Abbey Road* album cover.

Tommy reached over and pointed, 'They're all wearing my clothes except for George Harrison. He was always difficult, George. But we did make for him too.'

On another page was a photo of Mick and Bianca Jagger sheathed in Tommy Nutter on their honeymoon in Venice. It started to sink in. Tommy was *really* fashionable. This was a really good job.

He began telling me his life story, and I listened with rapt attention.

Tommy had lost his business in the early 1970s. He started again backed by Alan Lewis, who had bought the Illingworth Morris Group, originally a fully vertical Victorian company which used to farm sheep, shear them, spin, weave, then make and sell through brands.

Alan acquired the Illingworth Morris Group off Pamela Mason, who was James Mason's wife and who Alan was having an affair with.

Alan bought the whole empire for £2 million with the intention of doing a Gordon Gekko-esque asset strip then investing that cash into other new projects.

A week after the Illingworth Morris Group, he sold the Salts Mill, which was the golden goose in the company's portfolio, for a cool £1 million. Salts Mill was the world's biggest textile factory when it opened in the 1850s, and the founder, Bradford's very own textile tycoon Titus Salt, built an entire village to house his workforce.

At the height of its production around 3,000 people worked in the woollen mill, before it finally shut its doors in 1986. It was bought the following year by Bradford entrepreneur Jonathan Silver, who wanted to create a permanent exhibition of artworks by his friend, local lad David Hockney. Today, the Salts Mill is a thriving art gallery, retail and commerce space and restaurant complex that attracts visitors from around the world.

Alan was always keen to make a quick turnaround and he was well known for taking some wild punts. He bought a forest the size of Wales in Russia only to discover later down the road that he didn't own it at all. The money he made from the asset strips would be taken out to Russia to do a deal by a guy called Chalkie, who worked for Alan. The money came back because it was marked. Sadly, Chalkie did not. He got blown up in a 4x4 somewhere.

He had his own bank, the Anglo-Manx Bank – that's how far-reaching Alan was – and he was only 40 at the time. He had his own bureau de change (a business where people can exchange one currency for another) down on Edgware Road. Alan's approach to business felt very scattergun and, at times, seemed quite nefarious.

Still, despite his mercurial ways, Alan was a very enterprising man. Before the likes of creative directors like Tom Ford made a name for themselves, you had purely business-minded moguls like Alan, who knew nothing about clothing, but knew the machinery of business intimately. He was savvy enough to know he needed a recognised name in the fashion world to be a face for the brand.

He reached out to Vivienne Westwood, and he'd spoken to Paul Smith, who was in ascendance at the time but not the global powerhouse he is today. They both turned him down flat.

Alan also spoke to designer Tom Gilbey, aka 'The Waistcoat King', who earned that nickname because of the flashy waistcoats he made and wore in his salon on Sackville Street. Gilbey was always seen wearing pink cashmere jumpers, driving around in an ivory Morris Minor with red leather interiors. He was the first type of travelling tailor before trunk shows became a rudimentary arm of any tailoring business. Gilbey partnered with a lady called Serena Kelsey and toured around with a team of girls. Together, they made a fortune, until eventually Kelsey and her team became self-aware and ditched Gilbey, realising that they could actually do it themselves.

Alan eventually hired Tommy and gave him top billing with the understanding that someone of Tommy's creative calibre and connections could help develop the brand.

I thought it at the time, and I still maintain the view that Alan wasn't a very good person for Tommy. He hadn't afforded Tommy a budget for a shop refurb other than the shop sign and a small cutting room at the back. They didn't invest in any product. He simply assumed that slapping Tommy's name over the existing stock and having Tommy's name above the door, 'Tommy Nutter, Savile Row', would be all that was needed to make the place a success.

* * *

When I started working for Tommy, I was hidden downstairs with the tailors and the cutters. One of the first things I learnt was how to press a jacket properly. It was quite a menial and repetitive task, but I appreciated that I had to begin somewhere.

At the same time, I was delighted to learn that Tommy had requested a bespoke suit for me to be made in-house. It was low fastening and double-breasted in chocolate brown, with a fine cobalt blue stripe woven throughout. As much as I'd like to think that Tommy commissioned the suit to make me feel part of the team, I knew deep down that my Hepworth's interview suit repulsed him.

Either way, and even though Tommy was my boss, I accepted the suit as a token of our friendship, and I loved that suit. I wore it every day to work with the utmost pride and I felt quite the dandy walking to work each morning, revelling in the attention from fellow commuters in their drab charcoal two-pieces, looking me up and down unable to mask their envy. Until one morning, when the heavens opened as I made my way down New Bond Street and got completely soaked. My mad scampering dash couldn't save the drubbing I got from the merciless English rain and my treasured Tommy Nutter bespoke three-piece was wet to the core.

By the time I reached Savile Row, it had swelled up to the point of disrepair – or so I thought. Until I was informed that if I pressed it properly in the manner that I had been taught, the suit will be magically resuscitated. Hours spent invested in pressing jackets and trousers in a tiny basement had proved to be what any apprentice learning a craft might call my wax-on, wax-off moment.

On occasion, I was called up from downstairs to man the fort on the shop floor when Tommy went to lunch. The floorwalker was the role I relished because, at heart, I believed (perhaps with the hubris of youth) that I was a confident salesman.

The first time I was asked to take the wheel, a middle-aged gentleman wearing a green fair isle sweater walked through the door with the kind of look on his face that suggested he had expected to walk into a newsagents or a barber's shop.

'Can I help you at all, sir?' I asked.

'I'm just looking for a blue suit,' Fair Isle said, pumping out his chest and reasserting himself.

This was my time to shine, I thought. I pulled out bunches and bunches of fabric, furiously Rolodexed my way through every available one, showing the man every possible blue cloth that had been woven by man. The man studied them all, combing every other one with his fingers and purring like a cat perched on a hot water bottle. I felt that a sale was close.

My mind wandered off to the local Tenby news clippings that my mother would inevitably scrapbook: 'Timothy Everest: The King of Fashion from little Tenby in Wales Makes Good on Savile Row'. Maybe the local news outlet might want to come to Savile Row to speak to me in …

'Thank you, I've seen enough,' Fair Isle said, bringing me back to earth. He shuffled his way to the door. 'I'm late for a business meeting,' he said.

'Maybe I can send you some swatches?' I pressed.

'No, thank you,' he said curtly and left.

*   *   *

While my sales technique was still in its embryonic phase, I leaned on my A-level qualification in art to impress Tommy, surreptitiously leaving my sketches around the shop for him to discover.

Tommy used to have a little kneehole desk in his office, and on some of the days where he'd be called away, I would sneak in and leave little sketches for him to find. After a few weeks of this charade, Tommy came into the cutters' room.

'OK,' he said holding a wad of my sketches aloft. 'Who is the Easter Bunny that's leaving little sketches on my desk?'

I was at the back pressing a jacket. 'That was me,' I piped up tentatively, as a jet of steam spurted from the iron into my face as if to shield me from any bollocking that might ensue.

'That's pretty good,' Tommy said positively. He spread the pages on the jacket I was pressing, like a croupier spreads a deck of cards. He pointed at the one he liked the most. 'Can you redo that one, but just make the shoulders a bit bigger and make the balance a little bit lower?'

After a couple of months drawing designs under Tommy's tutelage, I was swiftly promoted to doing all the drawings and designs for Tommy's Japanese line in the Hankyu Department Store. Hankyu is a landmark terminal department store in Osaka, renowned for its luxury fashion outlets and high-end restaurants housed over two underground floors and thirteen above ground.

Years later, through these same connections and relationships that I forged and nurtured with the help of Tommy, I would establish my own licence with Hankyu and as a result, you still have Timothy Everest in every department store in Osaka.

Tommy was always very generous. Not only did he frequently go out of his way to introduce me to his connections, but he allowed me to hang on his coattails at social events. These included the high-end, raucous Elton John parties down in Datchet, just next door to Windsor

Castle. Elton had just launched his 'I'm Still Standing' world tour, and we provided him with countless boater hats and tailcoats in Prince of Wales check.

John Galliano was another great connection I met through Tommy. John came to Tommy's for a work placement while studying at Central Saint Martins College. It was through John that I got to know the Chelsea Cobbler, a hip British shoe brand that was burgeoning a trend in bespoke well-made, expensive shoes as a counter to the cheap mass-produced shoes that were flooding the market at that time. I was utterly beguiled by this brand and made a rather exorbitant purchase for some Oxford boots that would replace my spats shoes for evening wear to the clubs.

John was a laugh riot and would often have Tommy in stitches with his Mae West impersonations. It was through my friends and John's connections at St Martins that I eventually learnt the art of design and the craft of putting a collection together. But more on that later.

We became quite a tight-knit bunch while working at Tommy's. It was an exciting time, too. Tommy flew us all out to Florence for Pitti Uomo, a biannual four-day trade show where brands show off their latest collections for potential store buyers and male dandies get to peacock for the cameras. We witnessed something of a renaissance in fashion design, which was about to change the world of ready-to-wear forever. Versace was just making some waves and Joan Burstein, the 'Fairy Godmother of Fashion', had just discovered this brand called Armani. She would later be one of the first to stock John Galliano in her store, Browns, and is credited with bringing (among others) Calvin Klein and Comme Des Garçons to the UK. Jean Paul Gaultier was also turning heads in his own inimitable way.

Back in London, we'd all go out to different clubs, predominantly gay clubs, to get a feel for what was going on with fashion trends. If you didn't frequent the clubs, you'd have no clue as to what was happening. The night scene of London, the clubs, the after-parties, the decadence and the music was the influence; it wasn't just what you saw in a magazine. I loved being out, and although I was not new to clubbing, I was now keenly observing and studying not just what people wore, but how they wore their clothes.

It began to be all-consuming. Like any 20-year-old, my entire modus operandi was to get paid to go out and have a good time. My clothes and my looks were a conduit for me to meet lots of interesting people.

We were hanging out with students from Saint Martins, who had the world at their feet. Tommy, although he'd only just turned 40, felt he was a bit too old for our scene. However, to his credit, he was acutely aware of the impact that music and the club scene had on fashion, especially with the young demographic, having revelled in it himself during his pomp. He would always ask John and me to come up from the cutting room if someone like Rod Stewart came in, to make the business feel youthful.

Meanwhile, with all this going on around, Alan's PA Catherine and I had started seeing each other out of work, much to the chagrin of Alan. He didn't like the fact that we were having a relationship within the business, although we thought we were being very discreet and professional. This only confirmed what I'd thought from the beginning about Alan: that he wasn't a very nice man. He sneered at our relationship and bullied Tommy constantly. Once I decided I didn't like him, the writing was on the wall for me at Nutters.

3

Malcolm

In the clutch system, the device which the master cylinder operates is called the slave cylinder. Without a slave cylinder a driver would not be able to switch gears.

Savile Row was competitive, and I learnt a great deal from watching Tommy, but not in a way that was conducive to helping one get a career in tailoring. I wanted to learn how to cut jackets, not just press them or make them look pretty on the mannequins. Tommy wasn't a cutter, he was a designer and a salesman, and no one wanted to teach me how to cut for fear of having their place in the pecking order usurped.

This general apathy from my peers encouraged me to do work on the side. Back then, tailoring houses generally took a blind-eye approach to this kind of practice, as the apprentice gets to make their own mistakes but never on the company's time or ledger. However, in my experience as a managing director, I've found this theory to be very short-sighted and never something I encourage. If someone in your company makes a success out of it, then they're going to start running their own books under the table, syphoning away any potential revenue that would have ordinarily gone into the business.

This same off-book approach led to the demise of Johns & Pegg, which was one of the oldest tailoring houses on Savile Row. They had two cutters there who were profiteering so much from making for their own clients on the side that the business ran out of money and was forced to close.

I remember having drinks with the cutters, who gloated about how much they were making under the table. A week after the store closed, I met up with them again and they were completely baffled as to the root of their downfall.

'We simply don't get where it went wrong, Timothy,' they told me.

'Maybe it was because you two morons took all the business away?' I suggested.

Tommy never suppressed anyone's potential – and equally, that was to his detriment. He said to me reflectively one day, 'It was my mistake. I let downstairs come upstairs.'

At the time, that sentiment was lost on me, but eventually I realised that his generosity in helping others became his own undoing. The people he invited into the inner fabric of his business slowly unpicked him from his own company.

This whole ordeal felt very grubby and left me in a ponderous state of disillusion. Shortly after leaving Tommy's, I was offered a job to be sales manager of the newish Ralph Lauren store on Bond Street, which was run by a gentleman called Ole Peder Bertelsen, better known to his friends as Peder. Peder was a multibillionaire Danish oil tycoon, who thought the fashion business was undervalued and underdeveloped. He was an investment advisor to an oil company that had, as part of its investments, a Colorado ranch. The neighbour of that ranch was one Ralph Lauren, who wanted to buy the property and, in exchange, offered his European distribution and his London flagship store to Bertelsen. Peder hadn't even heard of Ralph Lauren before Ralph called Peder asking to sell him half of the mountain but he was strongly advised to take the deal and he never looked back. It was a very beautiful store, it's a Sotheby's now. I knew Ralph a little bit through Tommy and turned down the job on that basis. Ego. Pure ego.

Despite my heartbreak at Tommy's, I was still interested in brands, and was still very much in love with retail. Peder was disappointed that I wasn't going to join him, but he connected me with another London retailer called Malcolm Levene, who had a small boutique on Chiltern Street.

Malcolm had been schooled by John Michael Ingram, a British fashion designer who founded the John Michael brand and had headquarters on

Savile Row. John was a famous 1960s retailer himself and one of the pioneers of swinging London. It was said about John that, had it not been for him, Kings Road might never have happened. Luminaries such as the Beatles, the Rolling Stones and Peter Cook shopped in John's stores.

If you weren't shopping on Savile Row, you'd either be in the cult designer menswear shop Jones or Paul Smith's (both on Floral Street), John Simons in Covent Garden, or Browns on South Molton Street. There was Grey Flannel on Chiltern Street and down a couple of houses was Malcolm Levene.

Malcolm was one of the best salesmen I'd ever met. He had a head as round as a football and spoke as much with his wavy hands as he did with his mouth. He managed to convince me to work for him without even showing me the shop.

The shop was petite, to say the least, and it was brimming with clothes. His mother Sadie was a very suspicious little lady and guarded the till as if the crown jewels were locked inside. This was such a downshift. 'What the fuck have I done?' I thought. At the end of the working day, I was ready to quit. And would have done for certain, had it not been for the stern words of my father-in-law, who reminded me of the commitments and promises I had made to Malcolm to take the business forward.

'You've made your bed, Timothy,' my father-in-law said. 'Now you can't complain that the mattress is too hard after one night's sleep. You should at least try and make it work.'

My father-in-law is what the Americans might refer to as a straight shooter. He was right, of course, and the next morning I rolled up my sleeves and got stuck into the job. It soon become evidently clear to me that despite all the shortcomings the business had, and without Malcolm being a household name, it had a very good clientele. He would head over to Italy and snap up all the end of line clothes from designer brands and bring them back to sell in his shop.

Malcolm had a very unusual approach to putting collections together on the shop floor. He would meticulously group his customers based on their tastes and purchase history and push specially manicured looks to suit their needs. He always had the customer in mind, and it didn't come as a surprise to me to learn that he is now an image consultant reportedly earning up to $300 an hour. Malcolm's process for curating the collections eventually went out the window because he would just end up buying whatever the brands were pushing.

The suit was changing also. The flares had long gone, the lapels were still big but not exaggerated like the ones Tommy made, the waist was getting lower, and the shoulders were getting bigger. It was the age of the 'power suit'. Although there have been many iterations of the power suit from previous designers – Coco Chanel in the 1920s, Yves Saint Laurent in the 1960s – in the 1980s the power suit renaissance was born from women who sought mutual respect in a corporate world by adopting masculine traits through an androgynous silhouette.

Giorgio Armani drove these trends forward, and every other designer quite literally followed suit. Hugo Boss was another progenitor of the power suit movement and Malcolm had the foresight and was the first retailer in London to have a concession of Hugo Boss in the Belmondo cut. I adopted the look too, helping myself to a preppy, oversized bottle-green blazer with tortoiseshell buttons from the shop floor. For my own amusement, I paired it with a pair of knee-length shorts and brogues. It screamed camp, but it was knowingly camp.

Despite Malcolm having a good clientele, the shop was running at a loss. It needed someone like me to come in and rethink its direction. I oversaw all the window presentations, merchandised and influenced the style of the shop, bringing it up to date with a polished direction.

I leveraged all the skills I had picked up from Tommy. In lieu of a proper education, Tommy was my true mentor. He introduced me to all things art – Art Deco, Clarice Cliff (one of the UK's most prolific and important ceramicists best known for her innovative, colour-rich designs), interior design – and he made every subject deeply fascinating.

Malcolm, on the other hand, was much more commercial. He was truly a great salesman, and it was all done by intuition. No one left the shop with just a pair of trousers. Malcolm would put entire looks together, co-ordinating the colours and patterns, accessorising with ties and playing with pocket squares. He earned the trust of the customer because he knew not only how to put looks together, but what looks would work for them.

After the customer had been upsold into spending far more than they anticipated, they would invariably ask Malcolm for a discount. He always tapped them on the elbow and said, 'No, but thanks for asking.' And he would gift them one lowly pair of socks.

Our customers came from all walks of life. They were all interested in fashion obviously, but also enjoyed the trappings that came with fine clothes: namely luxury cars, exotic travel and very fine dining. Having a background in the food industry, I was always keen to follow up on every client invitation or recommendation to new and exciting restaurants. Through the business I got to meet a lot of people who would go on to be famous chefs and restaurateurs. Harvey's restaurant in Wandsworth, run by the *enfant terrible* of British cuisine, Marco Pierre White, became my regular stomping ground, although the prices were astronomical.

To this day, Catherine and I still talk about the bill we got for one piece each of lobster ravioli and some fancy-pants raspberry ice cream dessert, though you'd never dare complain about the prices in the restaurant itself. We'd all heard the stories of rich Americans frivolously ordering bottles of wine and then consequently being frogmarched out by Marco himself once they dared to protest about the bill. But none of this was considered a negative. Marco was a rising star, and it was all part of the Cool Britannia movement, where people in ordinary vocations were suddenly bringing an angry edge to the workplace. Nobody knew where the movement was leading to, but it was all coming to the boil quite nicely and business was booming.

We'd expanded the shop, taking over the next two units on the street. Seriously, we couldn't take money quick enough, especially on Saturdays. As well as Malcolm's clients, stylists had started to come to me, asking for entire wardrobes for their clients. MTV had just taken off, and now bands and artists had become more fashion conscious than ever before. There was also the film world that needed new looks.

I knew Tim Angel, who used to own Morris Angels, a sixth-generation costume house that has provided for every possible TV and film franchise that you can think of from *James Bond* to *Doctor Who*. It houses an estimated 5 million garments over 8 miles of rails, so you can easily get lost. The costumes can also get misplaced. One day, someone even rediscovered the original cloak worn by Sir Alec Guinness as Obi-Wan Kenobi just hanging unassumingly on a rail, nearly forty years since Sir Alec had worn it in the original *Star Wars*. That turned out to be a very lucrative connection as I would constantly be pulling clothes and sets for all their talent.

The commissions were explosive and with my newfound wealth I splashed out on a two-door coupe Mercedes and a Jensen Healey sportscar. Of course, although I was flush, I was permanently overdrawn. But that was just the way it was back then.

One month, my pay cheque had an extra couple of zeros added to the end of it. 'Malcolm,' I said, 'it looks like accounts have made a grave error in my favour. Unless you've decided to give me a place on the board, that is?'

Malcolm peered at my payslip over his small thin-framed rectangular glasses for all of two seconds before handing it back to me. 'No, Tim, that's for you,' he said. 'You've done a really good job. You've earned a little bonus.'

I went home pleased as punch. A week later, however, I discovered Malcolm had paid himself ten times that amount. Now with the benefit of hindsight, while the business was on its knees, I can appreciate that Malcolm probably hadn't paid himself a proper wage for years. But at the time, it really pissed me off. Although it wasn't until I tried pushing the boat out with the Malcolm Levene brand that we really fell out.

The Malcolm Levene brand was white-labelled goods that the other brands had supplied us with. For example, Hugo Boss would deliver labelled and unlabelled suits. The unlabelled suits were for us to put our own branding on.

The penny dropped one day when I was fitting a customer in a Hugo Boss suit. The customer tried on a Hugo Boss jacket, followed by the rebranded 'Malcolm Levene' jacket, still by Hugo Boss. Effectively, it was the same jacket. Same cut, same fabric, only the label was different. The customer put on the rebranded jacket and remarked, 'See, yours fits so much better?'

I told Malcolm about the incident and that we should be steering the business towards Malcolm Levene more and reducing the interest we were showing to other brands on our books. 'We should explore this opportunity,' I said to Malcolm.

'OK Timothy,' he said. 'Go away, put a collection together, and we'll see how things turn out.'

Putting a collection together is no easy task. Yes, I'd pulled sets for clients and for stylists, but putting an entire collection together is a different beast altogether. And talking of beasts, whenever I'd approach Malcolm on the subject, asking for advice and approvals, the more agitated he seemed to get.

This made no sense to me. I was 24 at the time and had no aspirations to make a Timothy Everest brand. My objective, my job, was to make Malcolm successful and play a part behind the scenes.

But Malcolm was becoming unbearable, and we eventually locked horns.

'What's the matter, Malcolm?' I asked. 'You seem very irascible every time I bring up the collection?'

'I'm not very happy with you,' he said.

'I gathered that. Shall I just go then?'

'Well, my name is over the door. Yours isn't.'

'I understand that Malcolm, but it's my job to put your name in lights. But if you want me to go then …'

'Yeah, why don't you go?' Malcolm cut in, calling a close on the argument and calling time on our working relationship.

He was very competitive was Malcolm, but he could also be very churlish when he wanted to be. And despite what he's gone on record saying to journalists over the years since, he is very risk averse. He had been deeply scarred by a previous failing in business and wasn't about to risk it all now by putting all the energy into pushing his own brand. Again, in hindsight, I can see why Malcolm was reticent to push the boat out further. He'd been waiting a long time to make money with the shop, and he certainly wasn't going to gamble that away.

But once again, Malcolm had really pissed me off. I had done all the work. The collection was ready to launch, and Malcolm had pulled the rug from under it at the eleventh hour. I was certain this would have been the right thing for the brand. Not to mention the brand was making money in no small part because of the direction I gave it. We built a very good team and I think Malcolm should have taken a step back, kept his involvement to a minimum with the fronting and the buying (all the lovely bits), and left the young team to make all the money for him. Instead, he hung around the shop floor, doleful and melancholic, and just became a very grumpy old git.

It was frustrating on another level because I knew Malcolm had many more skill sets left to teach me. With Tommy, I learnt how to pull looks based on the aesthetics of what we were seeing physically out in the clubs. With Malcolm, I learnt how to present a collection in a way that made it easy for people to buy and wear.

We were young, and we could bring in a different audience. We could have driven the business for him and who knows what could have come of that. But that argument with Malcolm was the breaking point. 'Fuck it,' I thought. 'I'm just going to go.'

I didn't know what I was going to do, but a few years out in the cold on Chiltern Street was enough time away from Savile Row to think upon it nostalgically and mentally erase all the negatives. I had a Louis Vuitton trunk in the back of my car stuffed with bunches[1] and I thought, 'Well, why not try a bit of tailoring?'

---

1   Books of small cloth samples.

4

Jogger Muggers

Three-point turns are relatively complex manoeuvres that really need you to have the clutch control nailed before you attempt them. Leaving the clutch alone and letting off the throttle is a better way for one to control the car's speed initially.

While I had hit eject on my career in tailoring, my career as a stylist was really taking off. Ridley Scott Associates called me up and I assisted them with some commercials for Citroën cars. Not a lot of people know that many of the big British directors such as Alan Parker, Ridley and his late brother Tony Scott all cut their teeth on TV commercials.

Tony, especially, was very good at the big car commercials. He always knew the best locations and could really make the cars come alive on screen. That's why *Days of Thunder*, a film about stock car racing that he directed, looks so sublime.

When you establish a good shorthand with your clients, you inevitably bypass any agencies or middlemen and work with them directly. Before the banking crisis in the late 1980s and early 1990s, the job paid handsomely, and I wasn't missing the retail life at all. For some of my clients who had special tailoring requests, I could always go back to some of the tailors I'd stayed friends with on the Row.

It was also important for me to project an image of success after leaving Malcolm's. Some of my clients might have thought I was a flash git, showing up to their place of business in my Mercedes, with my boot brimming with swatches ready to measure them up on the spot. But I was just looking at doing things in a new way because selling oversized Armani jackets was getting very wearisome. Tommy had always taught me never to imitate what other people were doing because you won't have a point of difference.

I've never been an academic. I am what I like to refer to as 'visually literate'. My education was ingesting the club culture and absorbing what I was watching on TV and film. One film that I enjoyed on a loop was *The Italian Job* – the original one, that is.

Doug Hayward was the film's tailor. He was a famous celebrity tailor who had made suits for the film's star Michael Caine in many films and in his personal life. He made for Roger Moore in his last three James Bond films and was even the model for John le Carré's character Harry Pendel in his book *The Tailor of Panama*. The film interpretation featured Pierce Brosnan, another James Bond, and the suits were supplied by Angels. It's funny how these things always tend to come full circle. Tommy had an outrageous style that I was into when I was younger, but I had an affinity with Doug's style. His suits were more wearable.

Doug had also made suits for Steve McQueen in *The Thomas Crown Affair*. That film resonated with me greatly. The film told the story of Thomas Crown, a wealthy young man buried beneath the trappings of his own success. Neither the Rolls-Royce, the townhouse, the butler or the French girlfriends can fill the void of his bored and dispassionate life. Subsequently, he turns to a life of crime to satiate his fix for adrenaline. And, of course, in those elegantly cut Doug Hayward suits he looked so very cool doing it.

Now at the age of 25 I knew I had to pull the trigger on what kind of career path I wanted to go down. I was too old to get back into racing and my only other passion was architecture. My close friend was a successful architect, so I sought his counsel and told him my plans of wanting to study his profession.

He said, 'That's great. You do realise it takes seven years?'

'I'm a quick learner,' I said.

'I know,' he said. 'When anyone else asks me, I tell them ten years.'

After a short resistance, I came back round to the idea of pursuing tailoring. I knew about styling, pulling collections, movies and I knew about the great institution that was Savile Row. But I wanted to rethink how I could make it work for me. How could we reach out to the consumer who's been habitually shopping at designer outlets?

* * *

Meanwhile, the club scene morphed into the rave scene. Bands like the Stone Roses, Blur and Oasis were feathering the cradle for the birth of Britpop. Everything was suddenly humming with activity. I would be getting texts from random people inviting me to warehouse parties in Shoreditch. I'd go to a few, but found once I got there, it would be dank, feral and littered with nefarious misfits. 'What the fuck am I doing here?' I'd ask myself.

It was during this time that I was asked by a former colleague to go out to New York and put together a British Ralph Lauren collection for a big catalogue business. The deal never came about but it was a great experience.

My friend Robert picked me up from the airport and ferried me straight to his place. Robert had gone out to New York to start his own business. He had (and still has) an amazing design building with an apartment terrace that capsuled all the decadence of late-1980s America. When I see *American Psycho*, I can't help but think of Robert's apartment.

He had a colour-coded system when it came to serving drinks, which consisted of yellow and red cups. It wasn't hard to remember. The yellow cups were for the highballs and the red cups were for coffees the morning after. After a heroic dose of yellow cups, stupidly, Robert decided it was a capital idea to chauffeur me around New York.

'That's where Lennon was shot,' he said, careering up alongside the Dakota Building. He talked fast and, like all great connoisseurs, spoke with infectious verve. 'That's the Helmsley building where they filmed *Arthur*.' Robert had an encyclopaedic grasp of all the pop cultural landmarks from film, celebrity and music. 'That's Columbia Studios or "The Church", as people call it. Miles Davis laid down "Kind of Blue" in that building.' My head was swimming, and the buildings and streets were coming alive as Robert seemingly wove stories of their provenance. 'That's the Chelsea Hotel. Sid killed Nancy there.'

Manhattan was wild. It wasn't just the kids who were populating the clubs in their Versace suits, it was all ages, and all dressed to the nines. I was wearing a very cool Jeff Turner leather biker jacket with big shoulders (Jeff would later become my first bespoke customer). I had black tracksuit pants, black Reeboks, a bumbag, baseball cap and a white rollneck underneath.

It was in one of these clubs that I managed to lose Robert. Naively, I hadn't written down the address and my phone was incommunicado the second I landed. Christ, where the fuck was I? My only chance of making it to Robert's place was by retracing the guided tour he had given me hours earlier.

'Which way to the hotel where they filmed *Arthur*?' I asked the doorman.

'Which one, *Arthur* or *Arthur on the Rocks*, the sequel?'

'*Arthur*, the first one. I think.'

There began my five-hour schlepp back through both uptown and the suburban slums of the Big Apple. While Robert had compiled a detailed guide to New York pertaining to all the relevant buildings and streets where various album covers, films and celebrities were shot, I had to now untangle the order from my pickled and hazed mind, which was a fog of highballs and whisky sours.

My head was also on a swivel for jogger muggers as I entered the Meatpacking District. Jogger muggers were a new breed of criminal. Yes, it's as daft but as real as it sounds – muggers who dressed like joggers!

Then came the moment where I became unstuck. I was entering Brooklyn, frantically thumbing through distorted memory files, 'Wait. We never went over a bridge.' Then, a jogger appeared through the 5 a.m. mist like an apparition. 'Jogger mugger!' I bellowed in my head. I spun on my heel and hurtled through multiple trash cans, ripping my black pants and sullying my beautiful Jeff Turner jacket with the remnants of discarded takeaways.

After unravelling myself from the wreckage, but now with a limp, I eventually found Robert's apartment building. The doorman eyed me up and down, my desperation ennobled with the smell of greasy chicken and piss. Despite my repeated pleas, he dismissed me.

I hid just out of sight, cowering inside an unlit porch, waiting for someone to leave the building. By now, people were getting up and going to work. Ten minutes later, the door swung open, and I ran like fuck, pushed past the gentleman exiting the building, slid straight into the elevator and panic-thumped all the buttons. 'Hey, you're not allowed to …' the doorman barked as the doors closed. I had made it. 'Wait, what floor was he on? What's the fucking number of his apartment?'

Eventually, and God knows how, I made it to the right apartment and Robert opened the door, holding a red cup, in his monogrammed dressing gown. 'What time do you call this?' he asked, though it wasn't really a question.

A short exchange of expletives followed as I brushed past Robert, and I wilted into the guest bedroom and collapsed. My bags were still at the foot of the bed, unmolested. I closed my eyes and thought about some of the places I had seen on my long pilgrimage back to Robert's apartment. It occurred to me that the Meatpacking District had similar industrial characteristics to Shoreditch and Spitalfields. It was certainly not a place to find yourself in dire straits at 4 a.m. in the morning.

My mind started drawing the dots between buildings, the scene, the cultures. I knew the buildings in Shoreditch that held the underground raves. Clubs like The Key or Bagley's, by London's King Cross, that on any given weekend could hold 2,500 sweaty strangers boxed in six tiny rooms off their tits (those warehouses are now where Coal Drops Yard is, a shopping district where you can buy fancy chocolates and over-priced hand-poured candles). I could see how the Meatpacking District also had that element of danger, but this gave it an edge and made it cool, much like any upcoming area before it gets gentrified, and the suits push the creatives out of their studios.

I wanted my own house. My own name above the door. Away from the West End. 'Make a point of difference,' I'd hear Tommy say. That was the moment – the briefest of moments – where I envisaged a clear outline of what my business would be like back in London.

And then I passed out.

5

Go East

The original Plymouth Fury only came in one colour, Buckskin Beige. If you look closely on the assembly line at the beginning of the movie, you can see *Christine* is the only Fury in cherry red, a sign of things to come.

There is nothing worse than having to stare at yourself in the mirror for a prolonged period of time, when you are still swimming in the vodka you had drunk the night before. I'd not long been back in London and was sat in a barber's chair down Northington Street, just off Gray's Inn, avoiding my own reflection by reading a magazine and rudely ignoring my barber Richard, who could no doubt smell the trouble gushing from my pores. Thoughts of creating my own space were still marinating. I wanted to move away from styling and move into tailoring instead.

The magazine had one of those irritating real-estate adverts that gobbled up eight pages between the features I was half-attempting to read. In this advert was a tiny column about a fourth-floor space for sale in a building on Dover Street. I knew that building because it had Peter Smith's Atlas Barbers in the basement and an opulent boutique on the ground floor run by a guy called Scott Crolla. Scott had impeccable manners and the sharpest cheekbones I'd ever seen on a man.

His shop was mesmerising, replete with Regency interiors, packed with deftly mixed chintz, paisley and tartan jackets, with brocade waistcoats and velvet monogrammed slippers. He had violet neon lights in the window (an idea that Tommy would later lift for his own displays) and he underscored a deliberately dishevelled look, retro-fitted for the classic English gentleman.

He had a great motto about subverting Savile Row fashion and selling it back to the yuppies. When I visited, I was in awe of how a shop could be a sensory experience as 'Musclebound' by Spandau Ballet poured out of the speakers and lemongrass incense sticks wafted down the aisles.

I remember once Simon Le Bon coming into Tommy Nutter's, looking for the Scott Crolla boutique. I tried to convince him that we had some cool stuff too, but once I gave him the right address he soon scarpered. Scott's shop folded in 1991, and Scott disappeared into relative obscurity. He couldn't even afford to buy back his own designs that Elton John had put up for auction in Sotheby's. He died of cancer in 2019, refusing all kinds of medicine and chemotherapy. Very sad. That shop is now occupied by Victoria Beckham.

With my new haircut, but still with a banging headache, I made my way over to Dover Street. Scott wasn't there, so I didn't waste any time. I pressed the tiny buzzer on the intercom that said 'Fourth floor', and it rang three times.

'Allo,' said a distorted voice.

'I'm Timothy Everest, I have an appointment.'

'Yeah, yeah, come up.'

I was buzzed in and made my way through into the Victorian elevator and pulled the shutter down. It didn't stop on the fourth floor; instead, it went straight to the top. The doors opened and I peered out into a derelict office that was completely gutted, bar a whiteboard with a drawing of two matchstick men engaged in a sexual act. 'Strange,' I thought. I yanked the shutter down again and pressed the number four. This time, it shot straight to the barber's in the basement, which had all the plaster columns removed from the walls. I gave everyone in the barber's shop a fleeting apology before ducking back into the elevator.

After several editions of this hapless routine, I finally deduced that in order to get off on the floor one so desired, one must press the floor button at exactly the moment the elevator approached said floor (they've fixed that since, which is a shame).

The fourth floor was teeming with Japanese larch and reupholstered mid-century furniture. It was like a hall of mirrors on one side and the smell of frankincense gave the place some additional exoticism. It was very eccentric. The music would jump from playing 'Pretty Woman' by Roy Orbison to Andrea Bocelli's 'Time to Say Goodbye', then back to Roy Orbison's 'Anything You Want'.

'What's with the music?' I asked the young lady agent who was showing me round.

'Roy Orbison died last night, so they made a playlist.'

Ultimately, I didn't go for the fourth floor, but I can always say I knew where I was when I learned about Roy Orbison passing.

Several weeks later, and no further down the road with finding a studio space, I was in the same barber's chair on Northington Street. This time, I was in a more chatty mood and told Richard the barber all about my designs for setting up a studio in East London.

'I want to get back into tailoring, but I want to be away from the Row,' I said.

'Why?' Richard asked, gluing tin foil strips to the tips of my hair.

'Two reasons. Overheads will be cheaper, and I want it to be accessible to everyone, not just the yuppies in Mansion House. People haven't spoken about British tailoring for years, and we used to be the world beaters when it came to tailoring. I see men still walking around London in ready-to-wear Armani jackets thinking they're Richard Gere. It's time for a change, it's coming. I can feel it.'

Richard taped another strip to my hair. The foil helps keep the colours separated when dyeing the hair, so it doesn't seep onto the natural, uncoloured hair.

'Do you want Medium Ash or Honey Blonde?' He asked, holding up two bottles that looked identical.

'Bit of both,' I said.

He applied thick dollops of both dyes onto a small, thin brush and combed it as delicately as possible over the aluminium strip.

'I may have something for you,' Richard said.

'I'm not going lighter than Medium Ash. That Platinum Blonde you put in last time made me look like I came from a *Smash Hits* cover shoot.'

Richard smirked. 'I have a couple of clients named Robert and James. They have got this derelict building in Spitalfields and they're in negative equity.'

'And?'

'And they're desperate to get some income for the building.'

I baulked. 'A derelict building in Spitalfields?' I said. 'Sounds like a money trap to me, Richard. There will be zero footfall, not to mention it wouldn't be an attractive location for my more affluent would-be customers to visit.'

'I'll give them a call, let them know you're coming,' Richard said.

The first thing one notices when they walk into any room is whether it comes with a roof or not. The roof at House Number Four on Princelet Street had collapsed in its entirety, its dead bones and guts composed of split balustrade and insulation, and of course, broken glass was scattered everywhere. The tongues and grooves of the wood floor panelling were all splintered and gashed, as if someone had attempted to pry them open with a claw hammer and given up halfway through. It was as abandoned and skeletal a space as I'd ever seen. At the back of the house were cement bags, nailed in place over the smashed windows. Not even squatters had taken refuge here. Yet there was something in its vulnerability and nakedness that appealed to me. 'This is so fucking cool,' I thought.

Robert and James had bought the place originally for £280,000 and they'd spent £40,000 'doing it up'. They had suffered some poor luck with the market crashing and at that time (1989) House Number Four Princelet Street was valued at £220,000 (Truman Brewery later bought it for £5 million and it's now an event space for filming and photography).

That same afternoon, I met up with Robert and James at their studio in a top-floor apartment in Great Sutton Street. Their studio was like something you'd see in those before and after daytime television programmes with every piece of furniture either made bespoke, refurbished or upcycled. Their front door was a cell door from a prison and inside, giant test tubes with filaments hung from the vaulted ceilings.

'Where did you find those, James?' I asked.

'Oh, I made those,' he said modestly, tucking both hands into the rear seat of his sand-coloured chinos. There was a huge picnic table in the corner made from mahogany floorboards that they had salvaged from a nearby theatre. In the far corner was a wardrobe with glass-fronted cabinets that they bought for a steal from the Science Museum. It was nothing short of intoxicating.

We worked out a deal for House Number Four over a strong cup of tea and a couple of ginger Hobnobs. I committed to a next-to-nothing rate, while they committed to doing next to nothing in regard to helping with the restoration. The area had a certain eccentricity to it that, as Howard Stern would say, was growing on me like a fungus. I could apply all my experience of working in West London and bring a left-field approach to an untapped East London clientele.

Journeying home to Southfields, through Spitalfields, lending half an ear to the murmurings of disgruntled market vendors shutting up shop for the day, I finessed the difficult speech I was about to deliver to Catherine. It involved curtailing any thoughts of matrimony, despite being together for seven years, and allowing me to borrow £11,000 against our flat for a punt on a complete ruin.

6

Build It and They Might Come

When restoring a classic car, some of the tools required will themselves require specialist training courses in how to use them. The one tool you'll need more than anything else will be a hammer, to hammer out the dents, and patience, to operate the hammer.

For anyone looking to renovate their own property, *Paint Magic* by Jocasta Innes is the book you need to buy. I had happened to stumble upon it a few years earlier when doing our own home improvements and it taught me everything I needed to know about paint effects such as dragging, sponging and ragging. In the hallway at House Number Four, the 1920s panelling had a rather crude mock-paint finish that I was able to replicate quite easily. To give the house some flow, I acquired some plasterboard and two-by-four to replicate the shape of the panelling as far as the eye could see, so if one were to go upstairs, one would think that it was a complete house.

We repurposed old toilets, wooden cisterns and gas radiators from the abandoned apartments below. I had become quite the accomplished handyman, doing all my own plastering, plumbing and even making my own cloth-covered electrical cables by weaving and stretching them to give them their natural drape.

It was a project that completely enveloped me. When it was finished, I allowed myself to wallow in a short self-congratulatory minute of a job well done. Only then did a cold shiver of fear start to trickle down my spine. It hung with that quiet, serene pause a driver feels when all their tyres leave the ground, a second before it cartwheels off the road. 'Hang on,' I thought. 'This is stupid. This is really stupid. People get nosebleeds as soon as they reach the other side of Holborn. Who the fuck is going to come over here to Shoreditch?'

The first neighbour I met was a bearded sculptor called Charlie, who had been squatting long enough in the flat opposite that he now had long-term legal possession of the property. When I asked him how he chose this street on which to squat, he replied, 'At the time, I found it to be the most depressing house, on the most depressing street in all of London. So, I must live here.'

To jump-start the business I assembled a little motley crew, and my first student was Hussein Chalayan, who I affectionately referred to as the new John Galliano. He had this crazy obsession about burying clothes in the ground with iron filings and then exhuming them months later for people to wear. He would later deliver on those ideas with his graduate collection for Saint Martin's College, which he called 'The Tangent Flows'. Mrs Burstein liked it so much she borrowed it for her window display over at Browns. If you bought Björk's second album *Post* back in 1995, that's Hussein's jacket she's wearing on the cover.

I hired a young set designer for tuppence. She was squatting in an apartment building across the road.

Our graphic design team were called Fuel. They were helping Tracey Emin, who had her shop just up the road on Bethnal Green. That was before she went to make her infamous 'Everyone I Ever Slept With' tent. She made quite a splash with that. Sadly, though, it was lost in the great Saatchi's East London warehouse fire in 2004 that also claimed fifty pieces from abstract painter Patrick Heron, which were cited to be some of the most important pictures to come out of Britain in the last century, sixteen Damien Hirst originals, and the early drawings of 'Captain Shit' by the 1998 Turner Prize winner Chris Ofili.

I still wasn't convinced bespoke would work for the East London crowd, so I had some ready-to-wear made. People eventually dripped through the doors as we continued to wax the floorboards. Our early customers were mainly ragtag raconteurs who, like me, had discovered the area through clubbing and were lured by the idea that we were cutting and making in-house.

My aesthetic was born of lack of capital more than intentional design. We kept the original fireplaces and furnished the rest of the house with cheap rustic furniture and beaten-up radiators. My house signature was framed by the concept of 'What if a Japanese designer did a minimal approach?' because that would save me some money.

I was also conscious that while I was trying to use the location as a catalyst for change, delicately persuading our West End customers to come and spend across town was not going to be easy. For one, the yuppie culture had gone. My customers who had previously owned Ferraris and helicopters had disappeared, although they did return when the economy improved.

At the time I was introduced to a young blonde girl called Alison Hargreaves, who had just moved to Hanbury Street to start her own agency. Alison indulged me while I immodestly explained the provenance of each cistern, each carefully manicured floorboard and panel, every hand-finished mirror salvaged from scrapyards. Finally, after enough self-promotion, I cautiously asked for her opinion.

'It's amazing, Tim,' she said. I knew there was a 'but' chambered. 'But who's going to come here? It doesn't make any sense. You're a young guy offering tailoring. We've got to do something about it.'

Some weeks later, we met again down at the Golden Heart, a Grade II-listed public house that stands opposite Old Spitalfields Market where Commercial Street meets Hanbury Street. East London creatives such as the Chapman Brothers, Sarah Lucas and Gilbert and George (aka the 'Brit Pack') were known patrons. Inexplicably, the ghost of social reformer Elizabeth Fry also reputedly lived in the cellar.

Alison and I drained a few pints of IPA served by Sandra, the legendary landlady, who would famously switch songs on the 'faulty' jukebox if they didn't meet her approval.

'Timothy, you would be stupid not to subscribe to some kind of PR,' Alison said flatly.

'I can't afford PR, Alison,' I confessed.

'You can't afford not to, Tim,' she said quickly, and cuttingly.

'I have some journo mates I can call.'

Alison slammed down her pint. 'Jesus, Tim! You can't ring up your friends and ask them to say nice things about you. It's simply not cool! You should be too busy making and selling the clothes to be chasing journalists. And if they're your mates, they can't tell you to fuck off if they don't like what you're pitching. You need a conduit. You need me.'

Reluctantly, I agreed to hire Alison for a nominal fee. Somewhere through the fog of teas and beers we burgeoned the 'new bespoke movement' idea.

'We've got to create the idea that something's happening,' Alison said firmly. 'Otherwise, it doesn't make any sense. We need to corral the best upcoming tailors in town that are not on Savile Row. Who do we know?'

Immediately, my thoughts turned to Mark Powell, who had a place just off Soho and was running a little club called Violets. His house signature was coined 'Gangster Chic' because of his throwback 1960s look and his early clientele, which included the Krays when they were incarcerated. A few months earlier, I'd seen him walking across Golden Square, just off Soho, walking into the same premises that I was considering taking on before settling on House Number Four. He had with him a very tall, handsome black gentleman in a lovat-green skinny suit, who went by the name of Ozwald Boateng. I thought I was the only one thinking about tailoring, 'If these two are teaming up, then I'm fucked'.

'If we're writing about all the other tailors, Alison,' I said, 'then they'll be getting a lot of free press at my expense.'

'You'll just have to shake hands with that, Timothy,' she said, gulping back a slug of Timmy Taylor's, as Slayer was promptly skipped on the jukebox by Sandra to the sound of a solitary groan by one deflated punter. 'But if we pull it off,' she added, 'you would get the recognition for spearheading the movement.'

'OK, Alison, as long as I get a mention in all the articles we place and the reviews of all the tailors are less charitable than my own.'

We planned it minutely. The first article we managed to get placed was in the *Sunday Times*. It was a silly-sketch article with me and another chap parodying Inspector Jacques Clouseau farting in a lift. It leveraged a lot of attention for us because Arnold Schwarzenegger was on the cover of the supplement.

* * *

When we opened our place, we felt confident that we knew what people wanted – we just had to put it in the right order. People wanted Italian colours, a slimmer silhouette and, importantly, their clothes to be made exclusively by us. To have anything off the peg would be like Marco Pierre White inviting you to his house for a microwave dinner.

From a financial standpoint, this also gave the business the injection in the arm that it needed. My initial investment of £11,000 was being quickly chalked off. With the bespoke element of the business, I could take a 50 per cent deposit on any item ordered, and providing I could deliver the goods within the set timeframe, I could get a credit from my suppliers. This would prove crucial for cashflow.

I recruited cutter John Byrne, who was working part time for Burstow & Logsdail. Leonard Logsdail would later move to New York and tailor clothes for films such as *The Wolf of Wall Street*, *The Irishman*, and *House of Gucci*, although Prada took all the credit for that.

John was going through a messy divorce at the time. He would clock in for work at 3 p.m., leave at 6 p.m. and go to a casino where he worked part time as a croupier. Still, he was the only cutter I could find who would come and help; everyone else thought I was bonkers.

Ready-to-wear still had its compensations, however. While I couldn't command Savile Row prices for suits made in East London, I knew that city suits were made cheaper because city tailors worked from a basic machine canvas that didn't require the craftsmanship synonymous with a Savile Row suit. I stumbled upon a workshop on Kings Road called Brother & Cousins. In no time, and for a very good price, we knocked out a City Line with cloth from Holland & Sherry to ensure the quality was up to scratch.

Thanks to Alison, we managed to sneak a couple of columns into the finance section of the *Sunday Times*. Next to a photo of me waving some shears with the obligatory tape measure around my neck, looking every part the authority on what it takes to look good in a suit, read the headline, 'The New Rock n Roll Tailor of Spitalfields'.

The next day, I arrived on Princelet Street to be greeted by twenty-five or so young businessmen queuing outside a derelict house, all wanting something a bit different from their suits. And the main difference they were looking for was the price tag. There was also a change in the mood music with business suiting at that time. It was no longer cool to be so flamboyant in the office. Flamboyant is fine when there is enough money sloshing around, but not when your clients are struggling to keep the lights on. Young men wanted to be taken seriously, which is next to impossible when strutting around wearing fat patterned ties and printed polyester suits. The British cut was making a comeback.

For the creatives, we offered a look that was inspired by the 1960s Guards officer, much like Lord Kitchener's Valet was doing in the 1960s, incorporating military wear into the modern-day wardrobe. Our take on that look came in pinstripes or windowpane checks, with bright-coloured linings so people would feel less square. We took that model and made velvet jackets in the Regency style. Being in the East End gave us that freedom to be a little braver than my West End contemporaries.

The piece in the *Sunday Times* permeated beyond East London. However, while the article flamed the interest for many people, it did not list my number or address. This spurred many a would-be customer to write and ask the editor for my details so they could come and get a suit made by yours truly.

One of those people would be Julian Richer, managing director of Richer Sounds, the UK's largest hi-fi retailer at the time. Julian was suitably annoyed by the omission of my contact details, and he carried enough cachet for *The Times* to write a follow-up saying, 'This is not an advertising page, but due to overwhelming demand, if you do want to contact Timothy Everest, here is his telephone number.' With that, we were off to the races.

My next big coup was to hire Alan Pitt, who had recently quit as senior cutter at Anderson & Sheppard after his application for the managing director role had been rejected. In a very British 'sod you all, I'm leaving' kind of way, he quit and migrated over to Burstow & Logsdail.

Alan invited me over to his house in Essex for afternoon tea with his very glamorous wife and two teenage children. Little did I realise that tea at the Pitts' was quite the event. Alan and his family had prepared a feast of lovely crustless sandwiches, speciality teas in the finest china and endless assortments of cakes and trifles.

'Where's your wife, Timothy?' Alan said, in his impeccable tropical worsted suit. I felt radically underdressed in my short-sleeve linen shirt and cotton twill chinos.

'I'm sorry, Alan. I honestly thought you were just inviting me over for a cuppa. I didn't realise you were going to all this trouble.'

We both laughed about it, and Alan eventually asked if he could come work for me. It wasn't really working out for him over at Burstow & Logsdail. I accepted his offer immediately. A bit of grey hair and gravitas was just what the business needed. With Alan on board, Timothy Everest started to look like a proper establishment; no longer a kid in a derelict house.

Things were moving quickly. One morning, I looked out my office window and saw Suggs from Madness parked up outside in his Mercedes estate with his kids in tow. He said he just came down to see what all the fuss was about.

Creatives from all walks of life dropped by, including the likes of Kim Knott, who was photographing for *Vogue* at the time. A few years later, Princess Diana asked Kim to shoot family portrait photos for their Christmas cards.

Eve and her boyfriend from *Casa Vogue* called in to have something made and fell in love with the building much like I had. 'We've got to put this place in *Casa Vogue*,' Eve purred.

'I'm flattered Eve, truly,' I said. 'But it's only a hall and two rooms. It's hardly the Palace of Versailles.'

'Don't worry,' said Eve, grinning, as she plonked in the rocking chair beside the fireplace. 'We'll shoot it to look like an amazing house.' And sure enough, they did. On the back of *Casa Vogue*, we got requests for even more interior shoots. We were featured in both *World of Interiors* and *House and Garden America* in the same month.

Everything was happening rather quickly, and the business was growing exponentially, without too much preplanning. Whether it was film work or being asked to collaborate with a Japanese conglomerate, it was all because of the magical aura that was being built around the brand. We rarely said no to anything or anyone, especially if it meant we were going to have a new experience.

My greatest asset, although I hadn't realised it at the time, proved to be my pure lack of business experience. I didn't know the hurdles that were yet to come. My naivety and dog-like devotion for refurbishing a residence fit for demolition should have been the end of my career before it even began. It wouldn't have bankrupted me, you can always come back from putting £11,000 on red and it landing on black, but had it gone sour I would have lost the trust of a lot of people.

The name was one of the few things we did think about at length. Why did we call it Timothy Everest? I'd much rather have called the brand pinstripes, or sharp suits or something equally as glib. But I realised the successful brands were living brands. Ralph Lauren, Giorgio Armani, these were brand names with faces behind them. That's why we called the business Timothy Everest. Plus, it made Alison happy – one less to explain away from a PR perspective.

In contrast, by the early 1990s, Savile Row, and tailoring in general, was on its knees in the UK. Savile Row had boxed itself into a neat little corner. All the tailoring houses were all stuck in their ways, all singing from the same hymn sheet of how their clientele all stretch back to 1922. 'This is 1992,' I thought. 'Why aren't you talking about the customers you have now?' All the houses lacked creativity when it came to thinking how best to market themselves into the modern world, and to a certain extent, they still do. It's imperative to have a point of difference in this industry. Competition is very healthy – as long as you have a point of difference. Luckily for the Row, people like Tommy Nutter, Ozwald Boateng and Richard James all came along at the right time and gave it some much-needed relevancy.

Around that time, I received a phone call from a gentleman tailor from a very established house on the Row. 'Hello, Everest?'

'Christ,' I thought, 'Is this my old headmaster?'

'This is Mr Fox.' (Not his real name.)

That's poor form. Clearly, Mr Fox had never been pulled aside and schooled as a young man like I had been, never to address oneself with a title. I brushed off the inflated introduction. 'How can I help you, Mr Fox?'

'You're doing rather well, aren't you, Everest?' he said, as if he was still trying to reconcile the fact.

'Well, we're doing quite well, Mr Fox, yes, thank you.'

'It's all this PR and marketing, isn't it?'

'I'm sure you probably know a lot more than I do about the subject, Mr Fox,' I demurred, recalling all of the deflection skills that I picked up from Malcolm.

'I'm sure I do, young Everest. I've been in this game for forty-nine years, man and boy.'

'Only one more and you'll get to wave to the pavilion,' I said, and wished that I hadn't.

There was a long pause on the end of the line. Finally Mr Fox showed his hand. 'So how does it all work?'

Years later, I was asked by that same tailoring house to be their managing director. 'What are you doing over in East London in that little shop anyway?' they asked. 'Why don't you come here and get a proper job?'

I politely turned down the position.

It was these variegated slights on my pursuits and endeavours to bring British tailoring out of the dark ages that drove me on. I sometimes think if we hadn't done it, and if Tommy hadn't reignited Savile Row before me, then it might never have happened.

These days, British tailoring has been considerably enhanced by the likes of Patrick Grant and Thom Sweeney. We were invited to launch a house on Savile Row, and I nearly went three times, but our clients regularly informed us that they didn't come to us for where we were, they came to us for what we did and who we were.

No matter what business you find yourself in, it will always be your customers who help you understand what it is that they want. It was my job to listen to the customer. Why weren't they being serviced sufficiently elsewhere? Why were they choosing me?

Once you imbibe all the feedback, your own DNA starts to form. I didn't want to be at the bottom of Savile Row's ladder, trying to climb up it. 'Let's build our own ladder,' I kept hammering to the team.

That's what we set out to do. That's what we achieved, and the New Bespoke Movement was born.

7

Mission Impossible

A good cruise control system accelerates aggressively to the desired speed without overshooting, and then maintains that speed with little deviation no matter how much weight is in the car, or how steep the hill you drive up.

David Bradshaw was a big-time fashion editor for *Arena* magazine, and he dressed a lot of high-profile people. He'd recently styled Michael and Janet Jackson for their futuristic music video, 'Scream'. It's been said in some circles that it was the most expensive music video ever made, at a cost of $7 million. David called me at my studio, as I was daydreaming.

'Timothy, I have something for you,' he said. 'But it's very top secret, do you get me?'

I placed my mug of Earl Grey on a copy of *Face* magazine, which had a black and white photo of Robbie Williams sticking his tongue out on the cover.

'I understand, David,' I said.

'They're remaking *Mission Impossible*, and I've been asked to assist with the wardrobe. Would you like to do it?'

Now, if the story of my life was ever made into a film, this would be the moment where the fuse would be lit, and the *Mission Impossible* theme (the original Lalo Schifrin version, that is) would kick in.

David had already sourced most of the casual wear for the film, including a very beautiful vintage Hepworth leather jacket. However, the film needed some tailoring. Enter yours truly.

'I'll pick you up tomorrow at 7 a.m., Timothy, and we'll head down to Pinewood. Bring your tape, won't you?' he said.

'Who am I measuring?' I asked.

'Tom Cruise. I'll brief you on the way.'

David and his assistant turned up to House Number Four the next day in a lovely chocolate brown 1970s Volvo estate with yellow interiors. We made it out of London in record time, and as we reached the A40, David's assistant briefed us on some of the guidelines to be adhered to when in the presence of Tom Cruise: one must not speak to Tom about religion; one must not discuss, either directly or indirectly, Tom's height; and we were told in no uncertain terms must one discuss or infer either their own or Tom's sexuality.

'These all sound very reasonable,' I said. I would later learn that these guidelines are never really set by the talent themselves, but by very sensitive and paranoid members of their entourage.

'Timothy, you should know that there was another fashion house involved before I called you,' David said, levering the indicator with the entirety of his palm.

'I thought as much,' I said, hoping he would elucidate.

'Donna Karan provided some ready-to-wear suits, but the shoulders are all, well … off. You see, Tom has bulked up a little for the role and now none of them are fit for purpose. Anyway, the wardrobe mistress asked if I knew anyone who could move fast and move well.' David honked at someone undertaking him. He grabbed the wheel harder, twisting the rubber away from the metal.

'I said I know just the guy,' David smiled at me. 'I know a hotshot tailor who can do it all in a pinch – and do it flawlessly.'

'I appreciate the compliment, David,' although I would have appreciated it a lot more if he kept his eyes on the road.

'I suppose you do know what this means though, don't you?' David said out of the side of his mouth.

'I've got the rub, David,' I said. 'If it all turns out to look like shit, I'll be the fall guy, won't I?'

David nodded, as did his assistant, who scribbled something down as if a verbal agreement had just become a written one.

Just as we rolled up to Pinewood, we got a call from one of David's assistants saying the schedule had been shuffled and Tom no longer had time to see us that day. A similar incident happened the day after – and on the third day as well, only this time David wasn't having any of it.

'This is fucking ridiculous!' he exploded, thumping both palms on the steering wheel. 'We're going in, Tim,' he said.

'We are?' I said.

'We're going to find Tom, and we're going to measure the bastard.'

'Fair enough,' I said. We both climbed out of the car and put on our aviators. Someone had lit the fuse as we made our way across the car park, the theme to *Mission Impossible* ringing in our ears.

We were instructed to wait by the changing rooms, which were repurposed from old Nissen huts, the kind you would have seen on an airfield during the end of the First World War. The galvanised finish on the curved steel t-section frames ensured this small village had a very austere and mildly threatening feel.

Each door had a sign that showed the name of the actor or actress to whom the hut belonged. On one door was a gold star and a picture of Elizabeth Hurley in that renowned Versace dress with oversized safety pins. 'Elizabeth Hurley is in this film?' I thought. 'That does seem like a curious casting choice.' (Later, I learnt it was Kristin Scott Thomas just doing a mini send-up.)

David and I had spotted Tom outside his little Nissen hut, sheathed in overalls with exposed padding. These kind of overalls are the stunt costumes worn by actors and would later be concealed by the costume designer. Tom was just wearing it because it was a chilly day. He busied himself by practising his lines as he paced with purpose up and down the sound stage. Invariably, he would pass David and me as he marched in and out of the building, clocking us with a suspicious eye each time.

Getting increasingly frustrated, David summoned me and his assistant into a three-man huddle where he divulged his cunning plan. 'We're getting nowhere standing around like lemons,' he said, and choreographed an ambush, placing us strategically in a triangular bottleneck so we could pin Tom in.

Minutes later, Tom came chuntering towards us, his head buried in a pile of papers that he was shuffling from page to page. I stood in my designated spot, mimicking the posture of an uncompromising bouncer outside a gentleman's club. It's quite an ominous feeling seeing Tom Cruise march towards you. He looked up just in time, turned on his heel, and got pinballed back by David's assistant towards his own changing room door where David was waiting. We quickly encircled him. Tom was trapped.

'Are you guys coming to fit me for the suit?' Tom asked.

'That's right,' David replied. 'Timothy here will measure you now, if you have time?'

I unfurled my tape like a yo-yo.

'Yes, of course, sorry. I've been really busy,' Tom said, rolling his papers as if to weaponise them. 'Let's do this.'

Once inside his changing room, Tom and I had a very pleasant chat about fabrics and what he wanted to achieve with the look.

'Tim, I just want it to look good but be comfortable at the same time,' he said.

'We can certainly achieve that, Tom,' I said.

'I'm not particularly tall, so please help me,' Tom said playfully.

I smiled. He had purposely eviscerated the elephant in the room, and in doing so, compounded my theory that it's always the busybodies who inflame these supposed sensitivities. In my experience, when you talk to the talent or client directly, they are less concerned – if at all.

Tom is actually not as short as people might think. Perhaps for a leading Hollywood actor, he has a shorter profile than most, but I would not describe him as short.

'We can make you look taller. It's about playing around with the proportion,' I said, running my tape measure from his shoulder to his wrist. 'We can elevate the natural waist so that the jacket can be a bit shorter, but not look out of balance.' I called out a series of measurements in inches and David's assistant wrote them down obediently. I bent down on one knee and wrapped the tape around Tom's thigh.

'Then we can make your legs longer with a pinstripe fabric and a slim trouser. You have quite muscular thighs, Tom, so it's important that we get the right shape there and taper it ever so slightly around the calves.'

'I've worked out for this film, Tim,' Tom said.

I called out another number and stood up to measure his chest. Tom needed no instructions to raise his arms as I looped the tape around his back.

'We can also do a three-button jacket,' I continued. 'But the buttons will be a bit lower than they normally would be. The middle button will accentuate the waist.'

The camera will also use clever devices so as not to pull focus on the actor's shortcomings. If you'll pardon the pun. The director of photography would position the shot so they could pan up and offer the illusion of height and also ensure that no lofty bugger would be in the main frame with them.

We made a beautiful three-button pinstripe suit and several skeleton suits[1] from a flannel by Holland & Sherry, a renowned cloth merchant who currently runs its operations out of Savile Row. We wanted the kind of fabrics that reflected quintessential Britishness, as this film was predominately set in London.

We got tone-on-tone shirts and pale blue woven-silk ties from Vanners, one of Europe's oldest and most prestigious silk weavers, who up until very recently had been weaving silk ties for brands such as Turnbull & Asser since 1740.

The shirt and tie look was paying homage to the original TV series of the 1960s, a series I very much enjoyed watching when I was growing up. Tom put his arm around me on our last fitting and said, 'Tim, you should have been here yesterday. I was jumping off stuff.'

'That's just a typical Monday for you, Tom,' I thought.

Jon Voight also had some input into his wardrobe for his character, Mr Phelps. He thought it would be cool in the climactic scene to wear a vintage cycle helmet in the 'hairnet' style, when escaping from the roof of the Eurostar onto a helicopter. It did raise a few eyebrows in the costume department, and many of us were not convinced this would be right for the character. After some pushback, poor old Jon

---

1   Skeleton suits are made from the same fabric but enlarged to cover any padding required for fight scenes or general stunt work – in this case, the climactic train scene between Tom and Jon Voight.

confessed his reasoning – he was just petrified of banging his head on something.

I managed to assuage Jon's fears by finding one of those helmets in a bike shop just off Lexington Street. The only problem was that it came in the colours of the Italian flag – red, white and green. No bother. We borrowed a permanent marker pen from reception and blacked it all out for him. He did seem rather pleased when I handed it to him. 'That's exactly what I had in mind, Timothy, thank you,' he said graciously. As with most films, everything has to be done in a pinch. Proving one's resourcefulness and thinking on one's feet is the key to earning a good reputation within the industry.

David called me one Friday afternoon. 'Tim, we have a slight issue,' he said, dispensing with the pleasantries. David's voice was completely devoid of humour.

'I'm listening, David,' I said.

'Brian [De Palma] has really put the willies up the costume department ahead of our trip to Prague. They need to shoot the black-tie scene, but most of the principal actors are now having to switch from single-breasted to double-breasted, and vice versa for the extras.'

David read out a list of multiples of jackets and trousers and asked if it was doable. The list went on and on and on.

'David,' I said, 'this *Mission Impossible* film is turning into the impossible mission for me.'

'Can you do it, Tim? We tried phoning round, but everyone is shut, and they all have to be made by tomorrow morning.' David was getting short of breath. The excitement was certainly getting to him.

'I can do it, David, leave it with me.' I rang off, gathered my crew and informed them of our very own mission impossible. 'But they can't be rubbish,' I said to my team of brilliant machinists. 'And it's imperative that we over-deliver, OK?'

My team pulled through, and this singular baptism of fire feathered the nest for all future relationships with costume designers, actors and film directors. However, my team and I were much more than guns for hire when it came to making costumes. We would have meaningful dialogue with all the principal crew about the fabric, fit and functionality. Rarely would anything be impossible, and never on a *Mission Impossible* set.

After the release of *Mission Impossible*, it really kicked off. David thanked me and asked if we'd like to get paid or have our name in the credits at the end of the film.

We were a tiny business still. We weren't DKNY and couldn't afford to give things away for free, so we elected to get paid. Also, I was never totally convinced that people watch the credits all the way to the end, certainly not back in those days. David told us to make sure we got some good notoriety on the back of our hard work. I put my confidence in Alison to place the story, and she didn't let us down.

We had a big feature in the Sunday supplement for the *Independent*. Some young girl was looking for a big break in journalism, picked up on the story and we got a four-page spread, which initially covered the *Mission Impossible* clothes, but then morphed into who we were and what we were doing.

Things started to go a bit bonkers on the back of that. In fact, the *Mission Impossible* coverage caught the attention of Elton John, who wrote me a card congratulating me. He was so happy to read about my success, especially as I was one of Tommy Nutter's protégés, who he remarked upon as being one of his best and funniest friends of all time. He finished the card with, 'I hope to come and see you soon'.

8

Vanity Fair

The Jaguar E-Type was launched in 1961 at the Geneva Motor Show and Enzo Ferrari went on record to call it 'the most beautiful car in the world'.

One day, we got a phone call from *Vanity Fair* saying the photographer Michael Roberts would like to shoot us on Savile Row. Michael was something of a trailblazer himself. Only a couple of years earlier, he had shot Vivienne Westwood impersonating Margaret Thatcher for the cover of *Tatler*. The editor got the sack a week later, although it was never confirmed whether the two were connected.

I made some phone calls to Mark Powell, Richard James and Ozwald Boateng, who soon became available when the name *Vanity Fair* was dangled in front of them.

On the day of the shoot, I drove down to Savile Row on my blue T5 scooter. Scooters were in vogue again, thanks to Britpop, which triggered the renaissance of mod culture. Films like *Quadrophenia* were being talked about again and the movement had become relevant once more.

We all filed in neatly around the same time. Outside Richard's shop, his window display was furnished by these beautiful sunflower ties, woven by Vanners, of course. Ozwald clambered atop a red postbox with the Savile Row sign behind him. The shot, which was used as a profile piece entitled 'London Swings Again', catches Ozwald looking insouciantly distracted. I also ensured that I was not going to be overlooked in my long lavender woollen overcoat and solid maroon tie with black Wayfarers.

The magazine cover featured Liam Gallagher and Patsy Kensit, shot from a birds-eye view, in a bed adorned with two Union Jack-covered pillows and bedsheets. Patsy looked electric in a see-through black bra, and it made for the perfect snapshot of sex and optimism that was welded to the upspring of Britain's youth movement at that time.

Northern Irish band D:Ream released the single 'Things can only get better' in 1993 and it became an anthem of sorts, the battle cry for the browbeaten working class. It went to number one in ten countries and the Labour Party used it as a theme for their successful election campaign in 1997. There was something in the air and Britain was rejuvenated once more. I thought to myself, as a nation we're not brilliant at everything, but we do excel in a lot of things, why don't we celebrate the things that we're really good at. One of the things we're very good at in the UK is British tailoring. We just need to take a fresh approach and make it cool again.

At the time, Brits were all too obsessed with making exotic bedfellows with European cultures, particularly Italian. Our cuisine became infused with rocket salads or tricolore pasta, anything with mozzarella, avocado and tomatoes drizzled in balsamic vinegar. Ferraris, not Aston Martins, were a must, if you could afford them. If not a Ferrari, then an Alfa Romeo. The James Bond franchise was tired and even when it came back with *Goldeneye*, it did so with an Italian tailor, Brioni, not Savile Row.

However, it did come back. All of a sudden, with the renaissance of modernism, revamped and reshaped under the guise of Britpop, people were looking less cynically at British culture. It was cool again. Dismantled Britain had regrouped and rediscovered its swagger. The needle had swung so significantly that people were quite proud to be British once more.

Savile Row must have thought it was Christmas with the amount of free publicity that was being generated for them, and it was all being filtered through us, in their little shops in Soho or derelict houses in Spitalfields.

At a client meeting a few weeks later, I bumped into a chap called David Lewis, a cloth merchant at Holland & Sherry.

'That bloody Ozwald Boateng,' he grunted.

'What's wrong?'

'His purple suits, his orange ties, those ghastly lime green shirts,' he paused to collect himself before continuing his unrest. 'What the hell's going on, Timothy? They're not even made properly. They're ready-to-wear! They're not bespoke.'

David went on, underlining his same misgivings about Ozwald. He kept circling, venting his frustration until he had verbally punched himself out.

'You know, David,' I said, 'the customers that you supply, Henry Poole, Huntsman, Anderson & Sheppard, they're never going to come to us. But while they're looking down their nose at Ozwald, they'll be walking into one of your shops, buying a suit and feeling a sense of affirmation. It's because of the likes of Ozwald and myself that people are talking about Savile Row again. Love us or hate us, you'll be the beneficiaries of that.'

Ozwald and I weren't having meetings every day on 'how do we become the coolest tailoring houses on the block?', but we had a point of difference and people have a knack of welding the word 'cool' onto something that reinterprets anything commonly viewed as acutely traditional. And at that time, no one was doing any 'cool' tailoring. Whether people realise it or give us credit, we've made a lot of difference. There are lots of people who've got into tailoring off the back of a business called Timothy Everest.

9

Paul Smith

In Formula One, team orders are issued to prevent drivers from racing each other, so that they conserve fuel, reduce the likelihood of mechanical failure and avoid a collision. Such orders have been made on countless occasions in the history of motorsport, sometimes causing great acrimony between the team and the disadvantaged driver.

Christopher Tarling was a tall man of full build, kept his hair swept back and understood the underwritten rule that a floorwalker in any tailoring house should always stand with their hands behind their back. One day, while working at Tommy's, I was seeking a pair of *Top Gun* Wayfarers but couldn't afford to pay top whack. I asked Tommy if he knew anyone who would give me a discount.

'If you head down to Browns and ask for Mr Tarling, he'll give you a discount,' Tommy said. On my lunch break, I trotted down to South Molton Street, all dolled up with spikey blonde hair, and asked for Mr Tarling. Christopher burst out laughing. Of course, Tommy had set me up. Christopher had never been referred to as 'Mr Tarling' in his life before I walked into Browns, I'm sure.

Christopher had known Tommy since he was a teenager and had even worked for him for a number of years. The glasses were £28.50, and Christopher granted me a £5 discount, which was quite a lot at the time.

Post-Browns, Christopher went to work for the company that founded Brutus jeans, a skinny-fit jean that became hugely popular among Mods, football fans and skinheads. They had a popular TV campaign and the jingle 'Jeans on' by David Dundas went to number one in the singles chart. They had a bonkers shop on Cork Street, where they ripped out all the original interiors and just made it white, and sold (as well as jeans) dressing gowns for exorbitant prices. It's an art gallery nowadays.

Twenty years later, Christopher and I were sitting next to each other on the new Eurostar, which was thundering back to London from Paris, where we had just come from a fashion show for Comme Des Garçons. It was held at the African Art Centre and was one of those rare shows where I was chosen to do some modelling. Chris was one of the other models, with interior designer Nicky Haslam, who had created the environments for clients such as Mick Jagger and Ringo Starr, third-generation tailor Charlie Allen, who cut his first trousers at the age of 11, and the McGann brothers. Paul McGann had just come off the back of doing *Withnail & I*, the soundtrack of which was scored by the same guy who wrote the jingle for Brutus jeans.

'Can I come and work for you?' asked Christopher, somewhat bashfully.

This came out of nowhere, but I was very keen to snap Christopher up. Having someone like Christopher is like having a great centre forward in your team. I knew it would give people confidence that they had come to the right place, especially as most of our clients were foreign to the east side of town.

'I think you're doing quite well,' Christopher continued, 'and you remind me of a very young Paul Smith.'

Paul is a redoubtable shopkeeper and was a big influence for me starting out. He had nice handwriting and his window displays were ornate, with artifices he'd imbibed from his travels. One day, I wandered past his shop on Floral Street and saw a beatbox in his window and thought, 'Christ, I wish I'd thought of that.' His windows were the physical manifestations of everything he was pinning to the mood board in his mind. We all got to be a spectator to that.

Christopher came on board and together we set up some meetings in Japan regarding licensing. Paul Smith and Mark Powell both had one out there already and I know Ozwald was also being groomed. Christopher knew Paul, and he told me that Paul was very keen to meet us and had invited us to his flagship store. In hindsight, I now suspect Paul was concerned that big business was rushing to sign up the licences in the same territories that he had already established himself.

Paul is a self-confessed hoarder now, but back then, I could already see him becoming a consummate collector. His office was teeming with all kinds of books, bicycles, toys and art of all kinds from around the world. He had the original floor plans for his Floral Street building framed on the wall. He hadn't even set foot in the building before he bought it in 1976, but because he has a mania for all things Bauhaus, when he was looking for a shop he peered through the shuttered façade and noticed that while all the other shops in the area were made of raw brick, this shop was made from concrete. The first minimalist shop in London.

After he gave me an enthusiastic tour of his collection, he presented me with an ornate wooden chair and a cup of jasmine tea, then he perched at the end of his desk, exposing his red and purple striped socks. 'You know I'm really inspired by what you're doing,' he said directly. 'The idea of a house of clothing is very original. It reminds me of when I was in the same grips of inspiration and passion that led me to start up all this.'

He gazed around the room, with a look that was just very slightly detached from it all. As if, despite all his beautiful souvenirs and belongings, they weren't satiating whatever itch he couldn't reach to scratch. 'I'd love to have a house to tailoring but I'm not a tailor.'

'You might not be a tailor, Paul, but you've already carved out a legacy that any British designer or tailor will aspire to,' I said.

Paul nodded and tucked a lock of hair behind his ear.

'Look,' I said, 'I've only got Christopher, who you know; an ageing coat cutter; a young cutter who smells of casino lobbies; two rooms in a derelict building; a very ambitious PR girl and enough money left for about six months' trading. But we're trying.'

'Who is your young cutter?' Paul asked.

Six months later, Christopher handed in his resignation and left to work for Paul at his new Westbourne house with tailoring on the top floor. It was a body blow for me, especially as I'd put my arm around Christopher with the hopes of exploring great new opportunities together. While Timothy Everest the brand was making headlines and gaining a lot of press, we were still only a small business with a young tailoring side.

Still, Paul was a powerhouse, and a very successful businessman intent on protecting his territory. He knew that swiping Christopher from under my nose would not only bolster his business but stymie mine. It was a big life lesson for me. Sometime later, John, the young cutter, also left to join Paul and Christopher.

Despite that mini-setback, Paul and I have always maintained a very good relationship, mainly through our shared love affair with cycling. He was a professional racing cyclist when he was younger, but like me had a nasty accident as a teenager which curtailed a career as an athlete and pointed him towards the world of photography, art, architecture and, of course, fashion. We've run into each other at various events over the years and he's always great company.

Without Paul Smith opening the door for us all and showing us all what is possible, we wouldn't have stood a chance. Conversely, without Tommy Nutter, Paul Smith wouldn't have stood a chance. You always need luminaries like this along the way to create opportunities and awareness for British menswear.

Dylan Jones (editor of the UK version of men's fashion and lifestyle magazine GQ from 1999 to 2021) would go on to write a book on Paul Smith and I'm in there, quoted as saying, 'If we're a nation of shopkeepers, then Paul Smith would rank amongst the best'. Paul wrote me a lovely note to thank me for that.

Big in Japan

From Samurai to contemporary Shinkansen, the Japanese have a long tradition of using the left side of the road. It will look and feel foreign to Americans, but the British will be quite familiar.

The Brick Lane Beigel Shop has been selling the world's best beigels since it was founded in 1855. On any given weekend, the bakery bakes over 10,000 beigels. One afternoon, I fancied one of their famous salt beef beigels and had one foot out of the door when I was greeted by six sharply dressed Japanese gentlemen.

'Can I help you?' I asked.

'Mr Everest,' said the eldest. 'We want to ask you, what do you plan to do in Japan?'

'I don't know, boys,' I said. 'You're the first to ask.'

'We think you'll do well in Japan,' said another.

'Well, I'm flattered. You know, I've never been to Japan. I'd love to go.'

'Then you should go,' said the elder firmly.

'Fine boys, sounds good to me. But I'm hungry now. Let's talk some more over beigels. You like salt beef?'

From that meeting with the sharp suits, I learnt that we were being courted for three Japanese department stores, two trading houses and an independent retailer called STRASBURGO in Osaka to license the brand Timothy Everest.

Licences are typically signed when manufacturers are seeking a popular brand so they can have production. The manufacturers then supply the department stores with the licensed stock at no cost to the brand itself. For example, Isetan, one of the largest department store groups in Japan, work on consignment and their main focus is fashion.

Let's take Paul Smith as another example. All of the Paul Smith product you'll find in a department store like Isetan will be owned by 'Paul Smith of Japan'. This mitigates a large bulk of the risk for both the brand and the department store. When signing a licence agreement, you also sign away how your product will be presented in the store. You also have no choice on your collaborations, but we'll touch more upon that later.

On our first trip to Japan, we were escorted around Tokyo by Junji Tajima, the founder of STRASBURGO. Junji must have been told as a young boy to 'smile and the world will smile with you'. When he smiled in your presence, it was like standing under a heat lamp in a cold beer garden.

He had come from a very wealthy family who made their money through property development. Junji, however, was only interested in clothes. It's a multibrand chain nowadays, but when I arrived in the early nineties they were just starting out and had their flagship store in Osaka. Historically, Osaka was the capital for clothing and manufacturing, although in the last ten years it's shifted back to Tokyo.

Tokyo is everything that you would imagine it to be but with countless aces up its sleeve. One can imagine the sushi bars, the flurry of people scampering under neon-lit signs at night, the brightly coloured 1980s-style Toyota taxis, but it's offset with many traditional historical temples, shrines and imperial palaces.

After our tour, I returned to the hotel to find out that a lovely lady who worked at the British Embassy had faxed through all the information on all the different companies to have dealings with that were in town. One of the names on the list they had highlighted in bold with an asterisk, saying, 'RECOMMENDED SUITOR' was the trading house Itochu. Itochu were the big boys in town and were looking to have a younger brand on their portfolio. It would be the more conservative choice, and their model for rolling out a licence had already proved successful for their other clients, Paul Smith and Richard James.

They had a manufacturer lined up who was willing to pay over £1 million to Itochu to sign us up. The next day, I visited one of their six factories and saw at first hand the quality and abundance of hand finishing they were doing for the likes of Chester Barrie and Katharine Hamnett, another Saint Martin's graduate. (This was before she terminated her own licensing arrangements because the factories weren't in sync with her own ethical guidelines.)

I've always appreciated someone who can communicate their personal beliefs and practices through clothes, and no one did it better than Katharine with her oversized t-shirts with large block-letter slogans. If you've ever seen the music video by Wham! for 'Wake Me Up Before You Go-Go', the white 'CHOOSE LIFE' t-shirt that George Michael is wearing is probably the most famous of her designs.

After a day spent inspecting the factory, we were whisked away down the Chikuma River to Nagano, a city surrounded by mountains which had just played host to the Winter Olympics. We stayed in this stunning family-run hotel that belonged to one of the Itochu chaps. For this trip, I had brought Marcus along with me, who had worked on our early collections as we were getting more demand for ideas.

Marcus was a tall glass of water with strawberry blonde hair and was the spitting image of the Formula One driver David Coulthard (although this was only made apparent to me afterwards when a Japanese colleague sent a promotional full-size cardboard cut-out of David to our London office having met Marcus on our trip).

We were greeted at reception by three elegant ladies in long floral tunics, who smiled and bowed in tandem before escorting us to our tatami room. We checked our shoes in at the door and entered another world. The room still had that greenish tinge and a scent of grass, that comes only when the tatami mats are new and fresh.

They handed Marcus and me two dark grey cotton yukatas (bathing robes). 'Fifteen,' said one young lady, and she repeated, 'fifteen, fifteen, fifteen', before exiting and sliding the door closed. When they returned, the girls exploded into fits of giggles.

'No, no, no,' the young lady said, cupping her mouth and trying to contain herself. 'You dress like lady!'

It was a small detail, but a key part of the Japanese etiquette is for men to wear the belt on their hips and for women to wear it on their waist. You're also meant to tie the robe left over right, which we hadn't done. The Japanese only tie robes right over left when they're dressing their dead. Although mildly embarrassed, Marcus and I were quite happy to be the hapless subjects of ridicule, as it further broke the ice with the girls.

They were still giggling as they led us to another room made of Japanese cedar that must have dated back centuries. Waiting for us next to some bamboo buckets, with their robes correctly tied, were the Itochu chaps. It was an uncomfortable passage of play.

'What do we do now?' Marcus asked from the corner of his mouth.

'I don't know,' I whispered. 'Just bow.'

We bowed, they bowed – and still no instructions were given as to what we should do next. It was like a blinking contest.

'Do we take off our robes?' Marcus said again.

'I wouldn't if I were you,' I said. I'll be damned if I'm going to disrobe first and find out that I got the wrong end of the stick again.

Luckily, our hosts led the way, and we all took our clothes off, apart from the girls, who wore small cotton bras and a short sash to cover their modesty. We submerged ourselves into the crystal-clear water that was so hot it caused Marcus to let out a tiny squeal. I paddled into a hot tub that sat beneath a waterfall and grabbed onto the sides, which were frosted from a recent snowfall.

The girls poured hot water over our shoulders and started to softly knead our necks in all the right places. It was heaven.

After the soak, we headed out into town for another great Japanese tradition, karaoke. My unashamed detestation for karaoke far outweighs my ability to feign polite interest in what I find to be quite a deplorable pastime. 'Don't you like karaoke, Everest-san?' Hero nudged, picking up on my frumpiness. Hero was one of the conduits from Itochu, a go-between of sorts.

'It's not really my thing, Hero,' I said. 'I can't sing for toffee, and neither can these boys by the sound of it.'

He paused, nodded, leaned back and exhaled heavily.

'Oh crap!' I thought. 'I've offended Hero with my indifference.' Karaoke was invented by the Japanese. It is woven into the very fabric of their culture, and here I was telling my host he can shove his country's greatest contribution to the world up his arse.

Then Hero's eyes lit up, like he had just discovered the answer to a crossword puzzle that had beaten him all his life up until this very moment. He leapt to the stage, wrestled the mic from another guy, who was murdering 'Come Up and See Me' by Steve Harley & Cockney Rebel, whispered into the DJ's ear and proceeded to sing 'Hey Jude' by The Beatles. Although, instead of singing 'Hey Jude', he sang, 'Hey Everest-san, don't make it bad … Hey Everest-san, don't let me down.' It was hilarious, and not only that, Hero could really bang out a song.

Early next morning, nursing some heads brought on by numerous nightcaps, Marcus and I came down for breakfast. The room was divided, the Itochu guys on one side and the chaps from manufacturing on the other. Marcus and I plonked ourselves down next to the Itochu guys, which caused Hero to leap over the tables and grab my arm in a fluster.

'Everest-san, you're not to sit with the Itochu people!' he said.

'What are you talking about, Hero? I thought we were all mates here; we all had a good time last night, didn't we?'

Hero looked stern. 'Everest-san, last night you talked about your business. Now it is their turn to talk about you and your business.'

Marcus and I begrudgingly sat down and dined alone on our traditional Japanese food, like naughty schoolboys waiting outside a headmaster's office. In our culture, I suppose that would be considered terribly rude to be openly spoken about, but it was just the way of doing business there.

Regardless, I had made up my mind that these guys were the ones to drive Timothy Everest, the brand, forward in Japan. It was the understanding of fashion and quality manufacturing that sold it for me.

Although my mind was made up, I had already agreed to meet Junji for dinner at a *yakitori* house as it was our last night on our first trip to Japan. That night, the restaurant was packed. The sound of sizzling skewered chicken and the frenetic chefs all clambering over each other at the grill like a horde of Romero-zombies scrambling over a defence wall, created a club-like atmosphere.

I had previously bought a book on Japanese etiquette, as I was keen to ingratiate myself with the locals. One of the things the book taught me is that you mustn't point your feet at your host. Ordinarily, for the average proportionally limbed individual, this would not be an issue, but for Mini BOD (me) this proved to be, quite literally, a feat of acrobatics.

Anyone who has been blessed or cursed with very long legs and a short body will attest that it's very difficult to cross your legs properly.

As I mounted the raised chair, I was cautious not to point my feet towards Junji who, as rotten luck would have it, had sat opposite. A round of Asahi beers were ordered and they arrived to a collective cheer from Junji's men. '*Kanpai!*' came the chorus as we chinked our bottles. I followed up with a short 'chin-chin' as an involuntary reflex, before taking a healthy wallop. Little did I realise that while '*Kanpai*' means cheers in Japanese, 'chin-chin' literally translates to your private parts.

Needing the bathroom, I excused myself from the table. I took one step and my legs buckled from under me as I spilled like a drunk onto the diners next to us. I hadn't realised that my legs had gone completely to sleep due to the lack of my own dexterity. 'So far so good,' I thought. Before we'd even seen the starters, I had successfully insulted the host, referenced my penis and the entire table were now guffawing at my apparent inebriation on only one swig of beer.

Calamities aside, the night went well, although I had to break the bad news to Junji about signing with Itochu. 'Junji,' I said, out of earshot from the group. 'I have to tell you that I'm being groomed by other potential suitors.'

He was crestfallen, and he didn't need me to tell him what he already knew. 'It's up to you, Everest-san. Do what you want to do.'

I felt bad. I'd extinguished that wonderful smile. However, he was very green to the business himself, so he must have known deep down that this was all something of a longshot.

My polite brush-off didn't thwart Junji's upward trajectory in any regard. Nowadays, STRASBURGO is right up there with other great Japanese menswear brands such as Beams or United Arrows. Junji had great taste, big ideas and powerful connections, but he was just too much of a gamble at the time I met him.

Back in London, we signed the deal with Itochu, who were a part of the ADO Group, an affiliation of the major department stores such as Isetan and Mitsukoshi, who, in turn, distributed the Timothy Everest brand. Itochu acted as the middleman between us and our manufacturer, Ohga Co. (this was the way things were done historically, although later we would work directly with Ohga Co.), and we started providing them with what's called the 'Know How'.

The Know How process, in its purest form, is a collection designed by the licensor (us), which undergoes several backs and forths between us and the licensee (Itochu). Once the licensor is happy, he or she would approve everything and sign it off. They then pay you a minimum royalty depending on sales. I learnt very quickly that this scheme was put in place to incentivise me to understand what sells not only in Japan as a whole, but also in the different regions of Japan.

Tokyo is quite conservative, while in Osaka (the peroxide capital of Japan), people are more inclined to show off their wealth with vibrant colours and cute accessories. Brands at that time were ploughing ahead with their cookie-cutter globalisation approach and not thinking native. They were trying to force-feed the same kind of look into every territory.

I adopted the philosophy that in every area there would be a different kind of Timothy Everest customer. Now, what collections would appeal to a Timothy Everest customer in South Korea? And how would that differ for a Timothy Everest customer in Taiwan?

I was completely green to the Japanese market. I'd already had a glimpse into that world through Tommy, who had his licence in the Hankyu store in Osaka, one of Japan's largest department stores. Each time the royalty cheque came in, Tommy would always present it to me with a huge grin and say, 'Hank Yu very much'.

In no time at all, a Timothy Everest shop could be found in over twenty different department stores across Japan, making us the fastest-growing fashion brand in the country. However, to put that into some kind of perspective, Paul Smith had around 200 shops at the time, making us rather small fry in comparison.

Today, the Isetan department stores in Japan (now Isetan Mitsukoshi) receive more than 200 million annual store visits, which is more than the total population of Japan (127 million). I was told, while visiting my first shop at the Isetan department store in Tokyo, that they had more footfall than Tokyo Disneyland. My shop was situated on the fourth floor, although I never thought of it as a shop, more of a concession.

Paul Smith agreed with me; when he saw his shops for the first time, he scoffed at the idea of them being called shops. The Japanese staunchly rebuked him, insisting they weren't concessions but shops in their own right. 'How much does it take?' Paul asked his Japanese board.

'About 1.2 million,' they replied.

It was phenomenal money, more than he was making on Floral Street, for sure. 'If it's making that kind of money, you can call it what you like,' Paul conceded.

We worked out very quickly that we had a slightly more premium customer than Paul Smith. We were catering for young executives who didn't want to conform and were almost strong-armed into wearing a suit. With that in mind, I designed the James Bond-inspired, shaken-and-stirred suit, suitable for both board meetings, cocktails after work and a fight atop the bullet train on the rare occasion one finds oneself in such a situation.

The bullet train is something every tourist should do when they visit Japan, although I'll always recommend to book ahead and be conscious of typhoon season. I'd fly over to Japan at least twice a year. Once, during the cherry blossom *Sakura* season, which happened in late March to early April and once in September, which was typhoon season. This would worry me enormously as I would fly into Tokyo.

On one occasion, I was on the Shinkansen bullet train from Tokyo to Kyoto when the train hollered to a screeching halt inside a tunnel. The announcement that came over the train's tannoy was incoherent to me, but the frightened coos of 'Typhooooo! Typhooooo!' that ricocheted down the carriages informed me of what was happening.

Because I hadn't made a reservation, I was forced to sit in a smoking car for four hours without any air conditioning. When I arrived at the hotel, the receptionist heaved. I stank like a pub landlord the morning after a lock-in. Thank heavens for dry cleaning.

We held several different licences. The licence still exists, although I don't own it anymore, but more on that later.

Our tie licensee was not only making for us but for Duchamp, and some accessories for Mark Powell. It would be common practice that you'd have the same licensee making for different brands and I was dispatched there to oversee production and ensure that everything was running smoothly. One of the designs I spotted going through their collection had been lifted straight out of my playbook.

'Go get Ebi-san,' I told the guide. Ebi-san was the manager. 'Ebi-san' was also a direct translation for 'Mr Shrimp', so the factory workers all called him Mr Shrimp.

Ebi-san rocked up, and immediately struck me as the kind of man who didn't have time to be held accountable for anything as tedious (in his mind, at least) as plagiarism. 'No, they are a different colour,' Ebi-san said firmly.

'Don't give me that, Ebi-san, a black-and-white copy of the "Mona Lisa" is still the "Mona Lisa".'

'We don't copy them,' he said, crossing his arms. 'We reproduce.'

'Is that right? How do you spell reproduce? C-O-P-Y?'

Ebi-san's face turned a colour red that would put a pillar box to shame. He stormed off, took a wrong turn down a short flight of stairs, stormed back up and out of sight.

The young factory workers were beside themselves, murmuring and chuntering. The young guide said, 'Everest-san, Mr Shrimp, he very angry with you.'

'He's angry?' I pushed back. 'How come I'm the one being ripped off, and he's the one getting the hump?'

Outside of the odd fracas, approval meetings were normally non-events – a dance that would consist of me looking serious and contemplative, invariably pointing and nodding at things just to convince the bigwigs around the table that I'm someone who knows what they're doing. Then I'd be chauffeured to the prearranged press calls, followed by a round of trunk shows.

The trunk shows gave customers an opportunity to meet with the designers and it was something that all designers had to do. For me, this was always the best part of the trip. I would help the customers pick out some pieces from the collection and then afterwards pose for the inevitable Polaroid. On the back of each Polaroid, I would scribble funny messages referencing something from our conversation.

Every year, for fifteen years, those same customers would bring those Polaroids back in and we'd all laugh and gasp at how young we all looked.

Me, in my slim gingham blue-and-white-check suit with my Britpop haircut and Patrick Cox wannabe shoes. (Patrick hit fame a couple of years before, when Naomi Campbell fell over wearing his shoes during a Paris fashion show for Vivienne Westwood. Still, I suppose when you design a 9in platform, accidents like that will always be on the cards.)

11

Saying Goodbye to Tommy

The most common reason your car may start then die is fuel shortage in your engine.

When I left House of Nutter, I was very upset. I filled out the duties on my last day in the shop, left the keys on the counter and quite unceremoniously said goodbye to everyone as if I was just taking the weekend off. I'd never felt so lost on Savile Row than the day I walked out of House of Nutter.

I went round to Stephen's salon.

'What's going on with you?' he asked.

My eyes were red and my bottom lip was already on the go. Without saying a word, I slumped into his arms and wailed the kind of tears you'd hear bursting out of a lovesick teenager. I didn't want to leave, but once I decided I didn't like the owner, the writing was on the wall.

I was very passionate about the business, and I felt very sorry for Tommy because his partner seemed like a bit of a bad egg. Tommy was not only my boss, but a great friend, and all I wanted was for him to find success.

We struggled to stay close after I left the business. When Timothy Everest got a big feature in the *Independent*, Tommy got a little sensitive about it. He wrote me a letter. Tommy always used to like writing letters. It was a very prickly letter, calling my collections a derivative of the House of Nutter, among other things. Reading it, I felt like it was a shot in the foot rather than a shot in the arm and I called Stephen straight away.

'Stephen, I've just received a letter from Tommy,' I said.

'Oh no,' sighed Stephen. 'What did he say?'

'Not much of an endorsement, put it that way. I've enjoyed better letters from traffic wardens. Has someone doubled his dose or something?'

'Look Tim, Tommy is not in a great place. I'll call him. I'll arrange for us to have a pint together.'

Stephen was always a great mediator, and we all arranged to meet at the Commercial. Tommy strolled in with his usual swagger.

'Hello doll!' he cried out across the bar.

We hugged the kind of hug you see when long-lost relatives reunite on *Surprise, Surprise*. He was wearing his bold black-and-white-houndstooth jacket and spats shoes. He gave me a kiss on the cheek and asked, 'Fancy a Judy?'

Tommy always called a lager 'Judy', after Judy Garland, who was rumoured to always drink lager in the morning before she moved on to vodka. We chatted about the big things and the little things, but mostly about the funny things that we did when we worked together.

Tommy was very complimentary about my new collections and wished me luck in the new business. A complete reversal on everything he had written in the letter. It was as if he had forgotten all about writing and the letter had never even existed.

As long as I knew Tommy he was always feeling under the weather. He was constantly getting colds and breaking out in all kinds of rashes. Everyone in the shop knew something was terribly wrong with Tommy, but no one knew what it was. We all knew about AIDS, but no one knew enough about it to take the correct preventive measures. We'd even morbidly joke about sharing the dirty toilet seat at work. But people started to pop off, especially in our industry. Halston, Perry Ellis, Gia Carangi, dubbed the world's first female supermodel, and of course, we all sat up and took notice when Freddie Mercury passed away. In hindsight, Tommy might have had AIDS when I worked for him, but it hadn't fully manifested itself.

He went downhill badly and quite quickly. He had become a recluse while he was ill. He told me a horrific story about him walking home to his apartment above Sotheby's on Conduit Street when his legs just went from under him. 'One minute I was walking, the next I'd collapsed to a heap on the ground,' he said. 'I couldn't work it out. I dragged myself across the pavement to the travel agents [now Hauser and Wirth] and they just thought I was pissed and left me there.' Tommy laughed it off, but I could tell it must have shaken him. Eventually, a tailor friend he knew passed by, grabbed him and dragged him back to his apartment.

When Tommy got really ill, he was admitted to hospital. His close friends and partner kept vigil and were there when I visited.

Everything you've heard about the horror of AIDS victims is true. Tommy was so emaciated he looked for all the world like he'd just escaped a concentration camp.

'Hello doll,' he said wearily, as Catherine and I walked in. His skin was shrink-wrapped over his bones and he was high on morphine. 'Jump on,' he said, slapping the bed. 'We'll go for a ride down the Thames.' We all broke out in tears of laughter.

Years later, I got a call from a chap called Lance Richardson, who would later release the book on Tommy's life, *House of Nutter: The Rebel Tailor of Savile Row*. He asked if I really did go to see Tommy by his bedside because several other people said that I hadn't. I asked him why would I make something like that up? If he didn't believe me, he could ask my wife, who was also there.

There were a lot of inaccuracies in that book, to my mind, particularly in the stories told towards the end of his life. Both Stephen and I refused to be in the book.

I was in the front panelled room in my studio at Princelet Street when Stephen called to inform me that Tommy had passed. I thanked him, put the phone down and almost on autopilot sauntered over to the Commercial for a pint at the same table we always drank. A lot of people came out of the woodwork when Tommy died, claiming to be much bigger friends and much closer to him than they actually were.

Tommy had his funeral in Golders Green Crematorium, but it was the memorial around six months later at St George's Church, not far from Savile Row, that really honoured the life of Tommy as I knew him – funny, quick and never a dull moment.

Cilla Black, who, along with her husband Bobby Willis, the manager of the Beatles' Apple Corps, Peter Brown, and lawyer James Vallance-White financially backed Nutters of Savile Row, got up and spoke about Tommy. He was joint best man at Cilla and Bobby's wedding. Apparently, when the priest read, 'Do you give all your worldly goods to Bobby?', Tommy whispered in Cilla's ear, 'There goes your Dusty Springfield collection', and they soldiered through the rest of the service in fits of giggles.

She regaled us with some very witty stories about Tommy. John Lennon and Paul McCartney invited Tommy over and played him 'Hey Jude'. Tommy sat in an armchair and listened studiously, strumming his fingers up and down the mug of tea he was nurturing. He would have been one of the first people outside of the band to ever hear 'Hey Jude'. After the song finished, John asked for Tommy's opinion, and Tommy told him flatly it was a load of old rubbish. He knew how to rile John and he quickly withdrew it, laughing, assuring them it would be a massive hit.

Cilla spoke very elegantly about Tommy and finished her eulogy by saying, 'Tommy was one of my best friends and one of the funniest men I've ever met. I'll miss him dearly.' It was just a great tribute to Tommy.

Deep down, he considered himself very normal, despite all the flamboyance and all the press that came with his high-profile lifestyle. He was never grand. He was probably too modest most of the time. Tommy often said he'd rather have a burger at Wimpy than be at the Savoy for a black-tie event. 'I'm just from a secondary modern from Neasden,' he'd say to me when things seemed to explode or spiral. Tommy never forgot his roots and that, above all else, was the biggest life lesson he taught me.

12

M&S

In 2011, the La Marquise (built in 1884, the same year that M&S was founded) was declared the world's oldest running automobile. It's rumoured that the La Marquise was the first racing car as the Count of Dion drove it in an exhibition in 1887 – although no other car showed up to race.

Ian Griffiths was an ideas man, and most of his ideas paid off. In 1982, an out-of-work Ian decided to study fashion when he was informed that Margaret Thatcher was considering conscription for the Falklands War. That was his first good idea. In 1987, he entered a competition to work at Max Mara, won, and has been the creative director ever since.

Ian was in his late twenties at the time, and felt he was grown-up enough to have an entirely new wardrobe of bespoke clothes tailored by yours truly. He was also a professor of fashion at Kingston University, so I suppose he needed to look the part.

He was always keen to align himself with people in the fashion industry so he could fast-track his students into employment at the end of their course. Ian could stream people very quickly into employment, with a placement success rate of around 90 per cent. He rubbed shoulders with the likes of Nike, Abercrombie & Fitch, and indirectly with Dewhirst, who was the biggest supplier to Marks & Spencer.

Ian called me in my office; I was in the middle of a salmon and cream cheese bagel. 'Hello, Ian,' I said, pleased to hear from him.

'Timothy. I might have something for you. You should be getting a call from a chap called Michael Terry. He is on the board at both Dewhirst and Kingston University.'

'Oh? And what do I need to speak to him for?'

'Well, he's a connector of sorts. As you know, Dewhirst are one of the lead sponsors of the placement programme here.' This made sense. Dewhirst wanted to employ the best people they could, straight out of university, so they could, in turn, provide the best product possible to M&S. 'Anyway, I was having a chat with Andrew Stone, he's the CEO of M&S, as you know. He's just tasked his supply chain with bringing in some "newness".'

'Newness' was one of those ugly corporate words invented by businessmen who knew everything about business, but nothing about clothing. Still, we can't have one without the other.

'Don't they have design teams in-house for that sort of stuff?'

'They do, to an extent,' he said. 'But here's the rub. It's mainly the supply chain, in this case Dewhirst, that helps generate the ideas to make it all happen.'

'That sounds like a very unusual relationship, Ian. The designs are driven by the suppliers?' I quizzed.

'Quite frankly, yes. Now, I was talking to Andrew, and I happened to mention you. You know, what with spearheading the whole tailoring movement, and I said you should be their tailor.'

'I see.'

'So, Michael will call and fill you in, and good luck with it all.'

'Thank you, Ian.' He had already hung up.

Sure enough, Michael called and invited me down to their head office, near Durham. They still had many factories there, despite moving some of their production offshore.

Jerry, my CFO (chief financial officer) at the time, was insisting that he came with me. 'I'll grind out the deal,' he would say.

'There's no deal to grind, Jerry. I haven't even made up my mind whether I'll go up there or not.'

'I'll grind out the deal, Tim. I'll button it down for us, don't you worry.'

'I'm only worried that you've been watching too many of those yuppie American films set on Wall Street.'

I called up my paternal chairman, John Hiscock. Whenever I needed some sage advice, he was always a good ear.

John was a contemporary of a gentleman called Richard Greenberg. Richard and John were knitwear merchandisers in the 1960s and 1970s, although John veered off to work on the manufacturing side and Richard went on to become the CEO of M&S in the late 1980s. A terrible car crash in his early forties nearly killed him, but he wasn't one to sit around and feel sorry for himself, so during his recovery he founded an agency that would enable young mainstream bankers to be more entrepreneurial.

During the early days of Timothy Everest, a lot of clients recommended John to me. He had a very unique understanding of how to structure a business, implement strategies and assemble a board. During our initial chats, we connected over our mutual love of *The Thomas Crown Affair*.

'John, is this the right move, do you think? Getting into bed with M&S?'

'What are your concerns, dear boy?' John asked.

'Well, I don't want to sound elitist, but we are premium tailors. There is a hierarchy, and M&S is a high-street brand. Why would I want to work with a high-street brand? It will cheapen us.'

'My dear boy, you are looking at this all wrong!' John cleared his throat. 'Think of this … collaboration, let's say, as simply you returning to university to finish a degree, but getting paid to do it.'

'Do you mean it could help with cash flow and I might learn something in the process?'

John allowed enough time for me to realise I had answered my own question before saying, 'Something like that.' John gave me a new perspective on how this collaboration could be mutually beneficial, although back then, no one was doing collaborations on this kind of scale.

John was very much the paternal figure for the company Timothy Everest. I miss him dearly. We played 'The Windmills of Your Mind' at his funeral and just like with those wonderful lyrics, you never just listened to John, he always made you think.

Michael's tour of the facilities was very interesting, but I wanted to poke my nose around in places he probably wished I wouldn't. When he finished, I asked, 'I'm going to take a wander round on my own for a bit. Is that OK?' And Michael agreed without protest.

M&S was suffering from a lack of vision on how to merchandise their products on the shop floor, yet I couldn't deny how shocked I was to discover the quality of those products when I viewed them in isolation.

For their Gold Label, which later transitioned into Collezione, they were sourcing the same beautiful Marzotto fabrics that I was using in my expensive collections. Only they were selling suits for £200 a pop. 'Bloody hell!' I thought, 'How have they done that?'

Most of the other collections were passable, but passable, in my book, is filed under 'boring' and 'what's the point?' They had some nice Harris tweed jackets, a throwback to the 1980s Continental look, but nothing was offered in a modern British way. What was really crushing the spirits of the workforce was the constant overreach of their department heads.

I spoke to an Indian man in the packaging department. He wore pristine cobalt blue overalls but with a rather dour expression. 'What's it like working here?' I asked.

The worker collapsed an empty chicken jalfrezi box in his hands, folded it to an inelegant clump and threw it with dead point accuracy into the bin behind me. 'It's a bit like buying a Ferrari,' he said, 'then finding out it only has a top speed of 30mph, and you're only allowed to drive around the block once a year.'

This was a big eye-opener for me. I assumed it would be difficult to get the go-codes for any out-there projects because of the endless bureaucracy. Whatever we ended up pitching, the powers that be were going to dumb it down. We'd have to aim high – always aim high. They'd beat it down, then we'd compromise at an acceptable level while offering some much-desired 'newness' for their customers.

On the train back to London, I sketched out some names for a label in my little black book. Only one name stuck, 'Sartorial'.

Back at the studio, I brought in my team to discuss the opportunity with M&S. Their main concerns mirrored mine before my trip up to Durham. 'Why would we work with them?' Jerry asked. 'They're high-street, Timothy,' he said condescendingly. 'They're not even a luxury high-street brand. They are popular, sure. Yes, they are a household name, but they are not premium.'

'Crikey, Jerry, you changed your tune. Look, I know you're sore because we didn't have to "grind anything out", but when it comes to tailoring, nothing irks me more than the elitism that comes with it. We have a chance here to change people's perception, make it accessible for everyone.'

I considered all the counterpoints, and managed to assuage the team's fears that there would be a conflict of interests. What we would produce for M&S would be a completely different price point to what we would sell to our Timothy Everest customer. I wanted to achieve a better 'high-street product' that usurped the competition.

Once I had my team on board, I then had to pitch Sartorial to M&S. I needed Michael to buy into my vision of creating an area that their existing customer would love and new customers would look to join.

'Timothy, this is going to be a logistical nightmare. You know that?' said Michael, as he hunched over his desk, inspecting my designs.

'How so?' I asked, gulping back one M&S orange cookie and squirreling another into my pocket for the train ride home.

'You want to do an entire collection, Timothy?'

'Yes, it's got to be a whole collection. Coats, knitwear, shoes, the whole shebang.'

'I appreciate you shooting for the moon on this one, but do you realise you're asking for the impossible? With an entire collection, you're crossing over into at least twelve different departments. It's not one seamstress putting all the coats and trousers together. How are we going to join the dots and pull it all together?'

'I'm just showing you the roadmap. You're the one who's got to remove the roadblocks.'

But Michael was right. I knew it was ambitious, and it was going to be a logistical nightmare. Getting Michael on board was the easy part. Getting the project off the ground took the best part of two years, but once launched, the collection was very successful in no time at all.

On the back of that success, I was courted to start a new collection at M&S called 'Autograph'. This was undoubtedly following in the footsteps of Debenhams, when they launched their 'Designers at Debenhams' brand in 1993. They had made it a huge success, enlisting the likes of Jasper Conran, Ted Baker and Ben de Lisi, who went on to make the famous red dress for Kate Winslet at the Oscars. They even got Kylie Minogue to do a line of home furnishings.

In response, M&S launched Autograph and signed up the likes of myself, Katharine Hamnett and my old friend Hussein Chalayan. They created a department in their Marble Arch store and gave us carte blanche with regard to the working brief. Their only suggestion was to create something new and fashionable, which was like telling the Head of Design over at Aston Martin to build a car that will get from A to B.

I wasn't hung up on doing anything new or fashionable. I wanted to put a collection together that would actually sell. I was looking at brands like Hugo Boss, who I considered the king of commercial success.

Hugo Boss released collections that were always on the right side of being fashionable without being trendy or boring. I leaned on the monochromatic town coats and knitwear that I'd just recently seen in the Helmut Lang collection in Paris, although there were rumblings that Helmut Lang sales had fallen off the face of a cliff since he sold a majority share of his business to Prada.

Fortunately, my 'Autograph' collection sold like hot cakes. Others didn't fare so well. Hussein, bless him, followed the brief to the letter but put far too much emphasis on the 'newness' element. His collection easily drew the most press because of its audacity. He couldn't get the collection off the ground, though, which is ironic really, considering the number of feathers he put on some of those clothes.

My collection sold, despite it being curated without any credible or creative taxonomy. In typical department-store fashion, they just heaped it on rail after rail, stripping it of all its glamour; much like one would organise one's washing on those foldaway laundry racks – quite neatly, and with the utmost precision, but in the dullest way you could imagine.

Later they released a new brand called 'SP' (short for Spencer). The 'Full SP', they called it. The concept made no sense to me. They were launching something new, but about to make the same old mistakes. I called up Morris, the head of menswear at M&S.

'Morris, it's Tim,' I said, brushing some bagel crumbs off my desk. 'You've already got a brand called "Autograph". It's a £12 million business, which is pretty sizable by M&S standards, but you're not managing it properly.'

'But we have traction, Tim,' he fired back.

'You have traction now, but the treads of your tyres will not survive another trip up the mountain. You didn't package the last one properly, and now you're going to launch another brand, "The Full SP". It's going to tank, Morris.'

'How do you know?' he asked.

'Because I don't even know what it is, and if I don't know, your customer won't know, and you'll need to spend a lot of time and money educating them. Also, the name is diabolical. "The Full SP" sounds like something a urologist will prescribe something for.'

I'm not sure if they were influenced by my indifference or not, but they shelved 'The Full SP', and opted to repackage 'Autograph' instead. Although they didn't move the colour palettes on enough from the initial monochromatic release, it still sold incredibly well.

However, M&S as a brand was getting merciless beatings by the media for moving more and more production offshore. To help them out a bit, I toured the country doing meet and greets, promoting 'Autograph' in all the major M&S stores. The journalists were very glowing about me and my collection, but they just couldn't help themselves caveating every review with 'the troubled M&S brand'.

We finished the tour with an elaborate exhibit in a casino, which was located inside a private club in the middle of St James. We installed a catwalk, illuminated by lights in the floor. I read in the newspaper, two weeks later, that the casino was forced to close its doors. 'The show couldn't have been that bad,' I joked to myself. Turns out, one of the patrons bankrupted the place, winning £2 million in one night.

After the show, I met with Stuart Rose, CEO of M&S. He was wearing his Richard James midnight navy two-piece, the sleeve heads elegantly roped, with a solid red tie and a silk blue on blue polka dot scarf. Stuart was very pro-Richard James, who I knew had been his tailor for a long time. He could have quite easily done his mate a favour and enlisted him to do 'Autograph', dislodging me in the process. But Stuart was smart enough to know that we were doing a good job, and we were making a difference.

'Brilliant show, Tim.' He shook my hand a little too vigorously. 'That was also very brave of you, going up and down the country like that. Putting your head on the block and talking us up.'

To his credit, Stuart backed us all the way, elevating everything we were doing with very creative advertising campaigns. He brought in more-seasoned faces to front the campaigns, such as Bryan Ferry and Twiggy, peppered with some younger guys and girls to bring in the younger demographic.

These initiatives were the brainchild of Steve Sharp, a lovely man and the same chap who created the pat-on-the-bum 'That's Asda price' commercials. We spoke about promoting 'Autograph' in my office one day. His voluminous blonde hair belied his age, which I guessed to be somewhere between late fifties and early sixties. 'He must frequent his wife's hairdresser,' I thought. 'It looks so unbelievably natural.' When the meeting was over, I had completely forgotten everything that was discussed as I was so transfixed by Steve's amazing hair.

After 'Autograph', M&S redirected their focus by sponsoring the Australia 2000 Summer Olympics. They instructed Dewhirst and, by proxy, myself (by this point, I was being paid as a consultant for Dewhirst, which meant on any given day I could be playing both the gamekeeper and the poacher), to create the look for the opening and closing ceremony.

The British Olympic Association flew Catherine and me out to Sydney for a press call. Princess Anne was there, along with the Northern Irish Olympian Dame Elizabeth Peters and two shifty chaps from MG cars. They were given a load of government money to buy MG outright, only they did a runner with the money and closed the company outright. The Chinese bought it in the end.

We checked into Rae's, a great little hotel on Wategos Beach, near Byron Bay, and made our way to the embassy for drinks. That was the first time I had seen the fruits of our labours out in the wild, so to speak. Sebastian Coe, the chairman of the London Organising Committee for the Olympic Games, in particular, looked very well turned out in the formal wear we had made him.

The parade was a different animal altogether. Typically, on a project like this, we need to be making the clothes six to eight months beforehand, but a lot of the athletes we were asked to dress were picked literally a matter of weeks before the Olympics began.

The casual look was achieved by working with fabrics that were easy to manipulate and a specific matrix that contained historical stats of thousands of athletes across all sports and disciplines. This system proved to be very efficient. A juggernaut of seamstresses and tailors toured the country and when the athletes who were local to Birmingham, Leeds or Manchester would be called in for a press junket, they'd get measured up and fitted.

The only variable a matrix of this kind cannot legislate for is people's vanity. On occasion, you would get the odd bodybuilder who would massage the measurements in his favour – a bigger chest here or a smaller waist there – but that was the exception to the rule.

As part of our trip, we also got to visit the Olympic Village, a true feat of architectural engineering. It was already designed to be a residential community after the games had finished. I was quite surprised to find so many fast-food outlets in the food court. I guess, once the hard work is over, why not treat yourself to a box of chicken nuggets. Judging by the amount of condom vending machines also dotted around the village, the athletes were also treating themselves to other leisurely activities.

The opening ceremony was something quite spectacular. The British athletes came out in our uniforms, which comprised the colours of the Union Jack – red, white and blue. The overall look wasn't entirely what we wanted to do, but knowing the amount of work that went into this project, the result was oddly gratifying.

Next to where we were standing was a large waterfall. At the foot of the waterfall, in an iridescent fireproof bodysuit, stood Cathy Freeman, an aboriginal athlete who marked the organisers' hopes that the games would promote reconciliation in Australia. She lit a ring of fire by her feet and the surrounding platform took off like a UFO borne to the skies.

'This must look amazing on the telly back home,' I thought. Some proud Australian bellowed behind me, 'How are you going to top that, Athens?' (Athens being the next hosts for the 2004 Olympics). Someone from the stands piped up, 'We'll put a kebab on it!' Which got a generous laugh. The Olympic cauldron was lit, but the water continued to flow, and was now beginning to flood the stands. We were forced to watch the remainder of the ceremony stood on our seats. But we didn't mind.

The uniforms we made for the games got a lot of mixed reviews. I've never really experienced bad press before, but I suppose with any project of this magnitude, it was always going to fall under much greater scrutiny.

Various journalists called me, scratching for any kind of quote. One journalist, working for the *Sun*, asked me, 'I thought you'd be putting them all in suits, Tim?' angling for a rise. 'Look,' I said, dunking a Bourbon biscuit into my coffee, 'yes, it was a compromise, but we're very proud of the final outcome.' My Bourbon snapped in two and one section tore off and careered to the bottom of the mug – unsalvageable.

'But why not put them in more formal gear?' he asked.

I carried on defending our uniforms, and while the journalist was perfectly charming, I knew all the while that he was going to fuck me. 'Still, better to play the game,' I thought. 'They'll write what they want to write anyway.'

Sure enough, the next day, on page 10 of the *Sun* the headline, 'Beckham's Tailor Strikes Back'. I did laugh, as initially I thought they'd used the word 'strike' as a pun, as that's the term given when the cutter will strike out the suit using a paper pattern on to the chosen cloth. 'Nah,' I thought. 'That's giving them too much credit.'

Off the back of the Olympics, I was invited to join M&S for a meeting with the Football Association. The 2010 South Africa Soccer World Cup was on the horizon, and M&S were commissioned with the job to provide the suits for the players.

I was in my office, eating a cheese sandwich that was just ever so slightly on the turn, when Michael called me. 'Timothy, we really want to do this. Will you come and talk to the FA?' He was very giddy and I could tell this meant a lot to him.

'I don't watch football. You could say I know sweet FA about football. Surely you can handle this without me?'

'We tried, Tim. We've taken one of your mohair suits and we've badgered it up a little. We had to show them something with a minute's notice. I hope you understand.'

'I understand; what did they say?'

'Terry has asked for you personally to come in and give the project some clout. You see, most of these footballers wear Dolce & Gabbana or Armani. Quite frankly, they think M&S suits will be ...'

'Will be what, Michael? Beneath them?'

'Yes, so Terry wants to ...'

'Who is Terry?'

'Sorry, yes. Terry is a high-flyer, part of 19 Entertainment, a management agency that looks after the Beckhams, the Spice Girls, that sort of thing. They have a sidearm company called 1966, which looks after footballers and brokers deals for the FA. Bit of a gamekeeper and poacher type bloke. He's been called in to broker the deal for Marks and Spencer and help the FA navigate through the mud of monies and the image rights, you get my drift? Anyway, he's asked for you to come in and add a bit of …'

'A bit of what, Michael?' I asked.

'Well, a bit of sex, I suppose. You know, come in and sex it up a bit.'

'Set up the meeting. I'll be there. And don't worry, I'll bring the sex.'

To say I was a casual Manchester United supporter would be an exaggeration, bordering on disingenuous. I really knew next to nothing about them, or any other football team. I thought it would be prudent to brush up on a little fan history of the club, in preparation for my visit. The general consensus among all Manchester United fans is that the most celebrated Manchester United goal was against Arsenal in extra time in the FA Cup Semi-Final match in 1999, courtesy of a player called Ryan Giggs who, according to the match commentator, carved through the Arsenal defence like 'bone through butter'. 'Done,' I said. 'Not that I'll be needing to recall any of that information.' But I committed the name and story to memory, just in case.

The meeting with Terry went well – it was a standard affair, talking colours, fabrics, making it look contemporary, all the buzz words that somehow had more clout coming out of my mouth than Michael's. The campaign they had in mind was also very interesting. It riffed on previous 'Autograph' themes, targeting both the older and younger generations. This time, we were going to make for the 1966 England World Cup winners, Sir Geoff Hurst, Martin Peters, Roger Hunt and Gordon Banks. The strapline would be, 'Four Legends, One Label'. And for the rest of the youngsters, Steven Gerrard, Theo Walcott and a bunch of other players I'd never heard of in my life, their strapline would read, 'Three Lions, One Tailor'.

'Brilliant!' I said, shaking hands with all the bigwigs. And went off for a cheese toasty in the canteen, with a cup of Earl Grey.

'Timothy. Just curious.' Terry asked, as I had one foot out the door, 'Who do you support?'

'Oh, Manchester United of course,' I said, with a wry grin.

'And what's your favourite Manchester United goal of all time?'

The blood drained from my face. 'Probably the one where that Welsh fella took his top off.'

'Ryan Giggs?' Terry asked.

'That's him.' It was the most vacant of answers. An answer that felt like a lie, even if it was true for every other Manchester United fan I asked. To try and claw back some credibility, I confessed my true reason for supporting the club. (When I was 12, I wore a horizontal-striped scarf, which was quite trendy at the time to wear with Oxford bags. Only later did I realise it was a Manchester United scarf. 'Never mind,' I thought. 'It's as good a reason as any to support a football team.')

Luckily, Terry and the FA bigwigs thought so too, and had a good laugh at the preposterous origin story of my football fandom. In unison, they asked me to design the clothes for the players going to the South Africa World Cup.

It was another great success for M&S – and a fairly simple gig. Peter Crouch was interesting. I remember, because one of our girls had to get on a box to measure him. They wanted to wear ties, so to give them a uniform look and to ensure they all tied the same knot, I put all the packs together and tied the ties around the neck, much like their mums would have done, I expect, back in their schooldays.

I didn't understand much about football, but I knew that just as we were asked to take care of their wardrobe, there were others employed to take care of buying their cars, houses or booking their flights. Nothing extraneous should take their attention from either scoring a goal or saving a goal. An entire infrastructure was built around them – and they still had spots.

Beckham wasn't playing in this World Cup, which would have been his fourth. Any chance of him being selected was thwarted when he ruptured his Achilles tendon playing in Milan, just months before. He left the pitch in tears, knowing that would be the end of his England career.

Still, he was on the sidelines offering his unwavering support. Whenever the camera panned to him on the bench wearing one of our three-piece suits, we would see a significant spike in sales. I was told at least 8,000 pieces a week would shift whenever Beckham was on the telly. But I'll touch more upon David later.

My relationship with M&S lasted for thirteen years, which was quite the run, considering we were only initially contracted to do one season. Then came a significant change in 2011, when Marc Bolland, who was touted as the 'Billion Dollar Man' because of the impact he had at his previous employer, Morrisons, succeeded Sir Stuart Rose as chief executive. Stuart Machin, who is the current CEO of M&S, confided in me his concerns of Marc. 'I hope he's not going to try and fix something that's not broken,' I remember him saying.

But that's exactly what Marc did. Marc was a trailblazer in the food industry, but his understanding when it came down to the business of the clothing sector was, for my money, left wanting.

Marc had a canny knack of constantly putting me in awkward positions. I was paid to consult and to come up with new initiatives. I would have teams and campaigns all signed off by the head of menswear or womenswear, yet Marc would never pull the trigger and instead would put up one roadblock after another, scuppering a lot of things that I was asked to do. We could have soldiered on drearily, but it was becoming an increasingly hollowing experience.

I was much happier with a new working relationship that I had just entered with Superdry because I could see the impact and the difference I could make to the company. But we'll have to come back to that later.

13

Oscars

When making the Ford Mustang, project design chief Joe Oros told his team that he wanted the car to appeal to women, but wanted men to desire it, too.

It was a typical cold, cloudy day in Paris and I had just left the Mary Louisa store on the nondescript street, Rue du Mont Thabor. We had a collection there and we were selling very well. The store was adjacent to the building where the anarchist Orsini constructed the bomb that he detonated in front of the Opera House in his unsuccessful attempt to assassinate Napoleon III. One block over was the Ritz Hotel, where Hemingway once ran up a bar tab of fifty-one dry martinis. I'm not a huge Hemingway fan, but I was thirsty both for some sightseeing and, no doubt, an overpriced alcoholic beverage.

Before I got there, my mobile rang with an unlisted number. 'This is Timothy,' I said.

'Timothy Everest, my name is L'Wren Scott,' said the lady, in a soft, but very commanding American accent.

'How can I help you, Miss Scott?' I asked.

'I'd like to talk to you about dressing Tom Cruise for the Oscars. Would you like to meet?'

'I'd be interested in having that talk with you, Miss Scott.'

'I'm in Paris right now, but I'll be in London in the next couple of days.'

'Whereabouts in Paris?'

'I'm in the Ritz Hotel,' she replied directly.

'I'm just around the corner, Miss Scott. I can meet you in the lobby in thirty minutes.'

'That would be great,' she said, containing her surprise.

'I'm wearing a heavy grey overcoat, cut snug like a military cavalry jacket. How will I recognise you?' I asked, pausing for a moment to get my bearings.

'Oh, you won't miss me,' she said, in a way I could tell was delivered with an ironic smile. 'I'm very tall.'

The round glass elevator in the Ritz pinged when it arrived on the ground floor. The doors opened and out walked L'Wren in a burgundy leather all-in-one jumpsuit. Being 6ft 3in without heels meant L'Wren had to duck as she did so, an act I expect she was well accustomed to.

We sat at the bar, and in the spirit of Hemingway, I ordered two dry martinis. 'I'm being employed by the Academy to be the stylist for the whole show,' L'Wren said, in a very matter-of-fact way. L'Wren was mingling with some pretty big people in Hollywood at the time. She knew the producer Richard D. Zanuck, who was famed for kickstarting Steven Spielberg's career and was Oscar nominated once himself for producing *Jaws*.

L'Wren was a real hustler in the nicest sense. 'Would you do something for Tom?' she asked. 'John Galliano is doing a lovely gold dress for Nicole Kidman. If you could make for Tom, that would be great. Although he doesn't want to wear a tuxedo. Do you have any ideas?'

'Well,' I said, lancing an olive in my martini glass with a cocktail stick. 'I'd put Tom in a beautiful dress-black barathea suit. It would be very neat, nothing extraneous, and a midnight blue tie. I know Tom. He won't want any bells and whistles.' I plopped the pitted olive in my mouth.

'Tim, I'm going to need your help,' she said, finishing her drink. She hadn't touched her olive, and I considered asking her if I could have it. 'I've got an awful lot to do and I'm not sure I can get everything done in time.'

'I'm at your service, Miss Scott,' I said.

'Please call me L'Wren.'

Two days later, I was on a United Airlines flight to Los Angeles. I met with L'Wren at the hotel, and we were escorted to Tom's house in a brand new Lincoln Navigator. Tom's gates clunked open, effectively dispersing a mob of fans, and our driver was instructed by L'Wren to 'floor it!' to allow security to close the gates rapidly behind us.

As we rolled up, there was Tom waving to me at the lounge window with that infectious Hollywood smile. He invited us inside, and we had a quick chat about all the little things in life that normalises situations like these. A buzzer on his intercom sounded, and Tom excused himself. I could hear him say 'No thanks' in the next room and he returned.

'Sorry, Tim. People at the gates.'

'More guests, Tom?' I asked.

'No. Someone saying they've come all the way from Italy and have some fresh bread for us.' Tom clapped his hands together as if we should get started on something.

'That's very nice of them,' I said, slightly bemused that Tom would turn down such a kind gesture.

'No,' he said. 'It's an old trick – they're just trying to "pap us".'

Tom and I had worked on three films together previously. The first two *Mission Impossible* films and *Eyes Wide Shut*, which was the last film to be directed by Stanley Kubrick. When he was filming in London doing *Eyes Wide Shut*, I would visit him for fittings in Holland Park, where the cast and crew were staying. We would talk at length about cars and planes. 'I've got a '93 Aviat Pitts Special back home that I'm working on. You've heard of those, Tim?' Tom asked.

'I have. The Pitts Special is a series of light aerobatic biplanes. They fly them quite regularly out of White Waltham Airfield, for training operations I imagine.'

Tom seemed pleasantly surprised I could hold my own on these topics. People in the fashion industry are not typically as well versed in mechanical vehicles as I am.

Back at his home, we continued to talk about planes and Tom led me into his conservatory, where he showed me his flight simulator. He was learning to fly a commercial airline, like John Travolta. Just as he was showing me the controls, his son Connor came in and asked us to watch *The Lion King* with him.

'Do you like *The Lion King*, Tim?' Tom asked.

'Yes, of course,' I said. Which was the truth, as my kids loved it, and I was more than happy to be subjected to it.

Tom put *The Lion King* on, and we all danced around the furniture to 'Hakuna Matata'.

Over the years, a lot of people have asked me what Tom is like. The first myth I always dispel is about his height: he is not as short as people make out. Perhaps for a leading actor in Hollywood he might be, but I never considered Tom as a short person necessarily. His reputation as a charming and polite gentleman precedes him and I always found his company extremely pleasant and engaging.

That said, and despite the several interactions I've had with Tom over the years, I'm not sure I've ever really met him. He definitely wasn't acting in front of me, but I always felt there was another layer that I couldn't get close to. Unfortunately, we lost touch, but I always consider myself very lucky to have met and tailored for him.

After the fitting, I left with L'Wren, shuttling through the gates and onto Sunset Boulevard. The roadside was teeming with banners promoting the 72nd Oscars. L'Wren was laughing to herself coquettishly.

'What's so funny?' I asked, grappling with a small bag of complimentary pretzels.

'This business is straight-up crazy,' she said. 'It's crazy I've even got this gig; it's too big for one person.'

'Well, I'm at your disposal, L'Wren.'

'Would you dress Robin Williams for me?' she asked.

'Sure,' I said confidently. I was less confident about opening the small bag of pretzels without them flying out everywhere. Conceding defeat, I placed them back in my pocket for later.

L'Wren gave the driver instructions and we drove into the valley to Marvin Hamlisch's house. He was scoring the songs for Oscar night, and I'd happened to call round when he was rehearsing one of the songs with Robin Williams.

Marvin was a very nice chap, but I could tell his patience with Robin was wearing very thin. Robin was one of the great comedic improvisors and was delivering a different performance each time. While this might be good in films and TV, it does not lend itself at all well to performing with an orchestra.

I sat at the far end of Marvin's lovely long conservatory, enjoying what appeared to be a private concert for my benefit. Robin was in full flow, singing 'Blame Canada', one of the Oscar song nominations from the *Southpark* movie.

I thought it was sounding marvellous, but Marvin was looking very disgruntled behind the grand piano. His brows started to frown to the same lines of his oversized optical glasses. 'Robin, this won't do,' he said, stopping mid-song. 'We've got to agree what you're doing. This is live television; you can't give me a different take each time because the orchestra won't keep up with you. If you shorten there, we'll still be going. If you lengthen there, we'll be finished and you'll be carrying on a cappella. We can all busk it, Robin, but we don't want to busk it on live television.'

Marvin was firm, but very nice about it, and Robin took the direction on board.

L'Wren commissioned a t-shirt for Robin that was emblazoned with the Canadian flag. The flag was lit up with LEDs powered by a very cumbersome battery pack that weighed so much it badly affected the drape of the cloth. Plus, some of the LEDs were intermittent, so we couldn't chance Robin wearing it for the whole performance. You do get to see the t-shirt briefly at the end of the final chorus when Robin whisks off his red shirt and jacket. It's on YouTube somewhere – you should dig it out, it's very funny.

Meanwhile, L'Wren was offloading more and more clients onto my books. 'I need you to make for Burt Bacharach,' she said, back in the car.

'L'Wren, that is quite literally music to my ears.'

Like most affluent Americans, Burt Bacharach had a capacious and meticulously organised walk-in wardrobe lined in cedarwood with custom-made ventricles. His wardrobe was complete with around forty pairs of pale blue-washed jeans. Above those, on hand-finished bronze rails, hung another forty or so white-washed, button-down shirts. There were a couple of barely worn tuxedos and a couple of neatly folded cashmere jumpers on the shelves above, accessible by a retractable ladder. This was Burt's uniform. White shirt, pale blue jeans and white sneakers.

During the fitting, Burt and I heard a commotion, causing us to look outside his window. Below us, parked split-centre of the in–out driveway and volleying the obscenest profanities across the hood of a limousine were Whitney Houston and Bobby Brown.

Burt let out an audible sigh. 'You'll excuse me for a moment, Tim, won't you?'

'Poor old Burt,' I thought, as I watched him wrestle them apart, file them back in the limousine like petulant children and instruct the driver to take them away. Because of that altercation, Dionne Warwick sang with him at the Oscars that night and not Whitney Houston.

L'Wren had other duties to attend to, so delegated most of the other fittings to me. Rather than hire a car to get round, she offered me her beautiful white Fastback Mustang, which had 300 bhp and was in absolute mint condition. I thought I was Steve McQueen, whizzing around West Hollywood. I rolled into a petrol station just off Sunset Boulevard. 'Cool car, man!' cried the pump attendant, three bays over.

'Thank you very much,' I said. 'Now, where is the filler cap?' I thought. 'I know about cars. I should know where the bloody thing is.' Fruitlessly, I inspected every single panel.

'Say,' I called out to the same attendant. 'I don't suppose you know where the filler cap is on this thing, do you?'

The attendant laughed to himself and strolled over with an almighty cocksure walk, as if he had been waiting all week for a moment like this. He folded back the logo and unscrewed the cap hidden beneath.

'Not your car, is it?' he said, feeling very good about life, and simultaneously eviscerating my Steve McQueen alter-ego.

The Oscars was a live television show, but it's run like a TV production. You'll have a director, a producer and someone doing the music, lighting and filming. Of course, there wasn't a stylist until the Academy hired fashion designer L'Wren Scott.

On the day of the Oscars, I was given an access-all-areas pass that expired at four o'clock on the afternoon of the event. L'Wren had my ticket to the evening ceremony. 'I've organised Tim to pick you up,' L'Wren said over the phone. Tim, another Tim, was her driver, who she shared with Ringo Starr. 'Tim drives a stretch Lincoln Navigator. The Navigator will stand out from all the limos. He'll pick you up, drive back to us and then we'll all jump in the car together.'

By 'us', L'Wren meant her and her professional date for the evening, the producer of the Oscars, Tom and Nicole Kidman and my plus one, who was the fashion editor for *Vanity Fair*, Harriet Quick.

To say that not everything goes to plan on Oscar night would be a huge understatement. I hadn't even left the hotel and my plans were already being scuppered. L'Wren called, 'Timothy, we're running late. Tim won't come now, so just jump in a taxi and we'll meet you down by the Shrine.'

'No problem,' I said, adjusting my batwing bow tie in the mirror. 'You have my ticket though?'

'I have your ticket. I'll see you shortly,' and she rang off.

The Shrine was the go-to location for the Oscars, Emmys and Grammys during the 1980s and 1990s. At the time, it was the largest indoor auditorium in the world with the ability to hold 1,200 on stage and 6,442 people in the audience. Outside of televised award ceremonies, you might recognise it from the 1933 movie *King Kong*, where the shackled beast is revealed to the audience in chrome steel chains.

There were enough limos outside the Shrine to cover a football field. I got out of my taxi and clambered slightly ungentlemanly atop a lamp-post in an attempt to see the Lincoln Navigator.

Just then, my phone rang in my pocket. 'Timothy, where are you?'

It was L'Wren. 'We've gone past the barrier now. Just meet us in the queue, and we'll all jump out of the car together when we get to the entrance.'

'My pass has expired. I won't be able to get through without my ticket.'

The line went dead. I approached the police barrier and pleaded my case to security that someone with a ticket was waiting for me on the other side.

'Sure there is,' the police officer said, with what felt like more smugness than sarcasm.

'Look, you can see my access pass only ran out half an hour ago. I wouldn't get dressed up for nothing, would I?

'Look buddy, no ticket, no entrance. Now beat it.' And just like I did in New York all those years ago, I pulled the 'What's that over there?' trick.

Except this one was more nuanced.

'Is that Clint Eastwood?' I pointed over his shoulder.

In the short moment it took for the security man to look left, I'd shot past him and run like fuck through the fleet of limos. I'd never seen a fleet of limos before, but here I was in my finely tailored tuxedo, running like fuck through them.

I could see the raised roof of the Lincoln Navigator ahead. It kept edging away, the closer I got, like the mythical pot of gold at the end of a rainbow. When I finally caught up, I landed both palms on the boot and thumped the window frantically. The door swung open, and I dived in caked in beads of sweat and distress.

As I was climbing in one side, Tom and Nicole were climbing out the other. It must have looked quite absurd to anyone looking on, seeing a man run like the wind to scramble into one side of a parked Lincoln Navigator, only to file out the other side behind Tom Cruise seconds later.

There was more security checking bags at the foot of the red carpet, and a line of people shuffling forward, waiting to go in. One of L'Wren's notorious character traits was that she never queued for anyone or anything. She marched right past everybody, A-listers included, which didn't take long with her tennis-court strides, much to the chagrin of Heather Graham and Ed Burns, who scoffed as they were not-so-subtly brushed aside. Under my breath, I apologised to everyone in her wake.

On the other side of security is where the real pandemonium begins. Joan Rivers and her daughter Melissa interviewed all the couples as they made their way down, past the press in the tiered seating where the super fans sat with their ticking list.

You've not seen anything until you've seen Tom Cruise work a crowd of super fans. He shakes hands and talks to everyone. Even after the interviews with every journalist from the Press Association, he'd pat everyone on the back, thank them for coming and ask if he'd see them later at the after-party.

My seat was four rows back from the stage on the right-hand side. All the big celebrities, like Jack Nicholson and Erykah Badu, were in the middle towards the front. In front of me, I had Ethan Hawke and Uma Thurman in that famous crimson Alberta Ferretti dress. Next to her was Angelina Jolie, who completed her gothic look in a black long-sleeved column gown designed by Marc Bouwer. She brought her brother James as her plus one and would later mention him in her acceptance speech for Best Supporting Actress for her role in *Girl, Interrupted*.

When Angelina vacated her seat to accept the Oscar, a looky-likey, in exactly the same dress with the same long black hair and arm tattoos, dove into her seat. This is for the sake of continuity. All the nominees had their own 'Oscar stunt double' waiting in the back of the auditorium ready to replenish their seat, because one can't have an empty chair when the camera pans back to your sobbing spouses, relatives or co-stars.

Behind me was Val Kilmer and Burt Bacharach's wife. Burt looked immaculate on stage in his midnight blue tuxedo that I had made for him, and I got to see first-hand how dynamic Marvin Hamlisch was conducting the orchestra. I had dressed the rest of his band in silvery mohair suits from M&S and tinted violet Cutler & Gross glasses.

Whenever they cut to commercials, I would call L'Wren, who was backstage, and give her a field report on anything that might need fixing on the presenters. Luckily, commercial breaks in America are quite long so we had ample time to tweak a trouser cuff or fix a bow tie here or there.

After the ceremony was over, I was still frantically running around doing errands for L'Wren. It was like something out of a Jason Bourne film, where I'd be receiving orders over the phone that sounded like they were a matter of life or death. Although, instead of being told how to get to the roof to escape any would-be assassin, I was told to find James Coburn and repoint his polka-dot pocket square, pronto. On one of my mazy runs, I ran smack bang into a lady in a full-length white dress, knocking her to the ground like an A-board blown over in a hailstorm – fully flat.

'I'm frightfully sorry!' I said, picking her up and dusting down her satin sleeves.

'That's quite alright, young man,' she said, removing her oval sunglasses. It was Faye Dunaway. *The* Faye Dunaway.

I remembered Tommy telling me she could be quite a difficult lady. She was married to Terry O'Neill, the famous English photographer, during the 1980s. In fact, one of the most famous Oscar photos you might see would be one of Terry's. A few years before he married Faye, he snapped her sat on a sun lounger by the swimming pool at the Beverly Hills Hotel in Los Angeles. Her Best Actress Oscar was on the black ceramic circular table, with the rather inelegant concrete tiled floor littered with newspapers telling the story of the Oscar wins from the night before. But she was perfectly sweet that night and very forgiving of my clumsiness.

I got paid for my time and all the garments that I was asked to make. However, there was never a budget offered by the Academy to dress people beyond those who are employed for the actual show. That's down to people profiting from the relationships with brands and fashion houses that they've either nurtured over the years or have been an ambassador for in years gone by. The red carpet is a different beast altogether and the budgets for those alone can be astronomical.

One gentleman, who was a well-known actor, was a close friend of Nino Cerruti. He would come see us at L'Wren's studio to be fitted and we would have a rail of Nino Cerruti tuxedos in his size waiting for him to pick one that would be a gift to him.

Many years later, I got a phone call from L'Wren. It was a business call and we discussed something with regard to her collection for Bergdorf Goodman. The details of the call were nothing of great importance, but the tone of the call stayed with me. There was something uneasy about it. Not so much in what was said, perhaps more in what wasn't said. When I put the phone down, I turned to my daughter and said, 'Something's not quite right there.'

The following week, L'Wren took her own life. It was St Patrick's Day, 17 March 2014, and she was 49 years old. She didn't leave a note.

I was too upset to go to the funeral. In hindsight, I should have gone. I was also feeling quite sorry for myself and rather angry that I had picked up on something but never followed through with checking it. I should have gone and seen her or called her – or something.

When I think of her now, I see her dancing on the spot beside me, just off the stage at the Staples Center in Newark, watching Mick perform with the Rolling Stones. He would sing right to her.

I still remember how happy she was with how everything turned out that night at the Oscars. When the curtain came down, she was finally able to relax. She gave me a big kiss and a huge hug and with the widest smile you could ever see, said, 'Gucci, eat your heart out.'

'L'Wren, I have to be honest. All the suits I had made were only about £200 from Marks and Spencer.'

She looked at me searchingly for a second before she burst out laughing, 'You're so funny, Tim.'

Left: If these streets could talk.
(All photographs © Peter Brooker)

Below: MBE pattern papers.

Left: My head cutter and trusted confidant for over twenty years, Lloyd Forrester.

Below: Inspecting Lloyd's handiwork.

OK, enough posing Lloyd – back to work!

A lovingly restored Georgian house at 32 Elder Street that was home to Timothy Everest's Bespoke atelier for over twenty-five years.

Left: The Golden Heart, opposite Old Spitalfields Market, refuge for East London creatives and home of legendary landlady Sandra.

Below: House Number 4 Princelet Street, where it all began.

'Did I leave the iron on?'

'If your name's not down, etc.'

I'm quite beside myself at our studio in Grey Flannel on Chiltern Street.

14

DAKS

Driving an overheated car puts additional strain on the engine, leading to further damage and costly repairs down the road.

One afternoon in 1999, I was in my office, neatly arranging an assortment of Bourbon biscuits in a Jenga-style tower on my desk when the phone rang. An assured voice said, 'Timothy, it's Jeremy Franks here.' Jeremy was known in the trade as being a true visionary and one of the best marketers in the business. He spoke French and German and was the chief executive and managing director of DAKS Simpson Group and a director of Sankyo Seiko. They had acquired the share capital by this point.

DAKS is a British luxury fashion house with a proud history that goes back over 100 years. One may be familiar with the name DAKS as the creator of the DAKS waistband, which was born out of necessity by the son of the company's founder, Alexander Simpson.

Alexander was a sportsman who sought a self-supporting trouser because braces could not move with the torso during a golf swing and belts bit into the stomach. Alexander dispensed with the braces and belts altogether and instead sewed rubbery tabs on the inside of the waistband of his trousers. He coined these new trousers DAKS. There are some conflicting stories around the etymology of the name DAKS, but the most popular one is that it is a combination of the word 'Dad' and 'Slacks'. If you look closely, you'll see the likes of Sean Connery wearing these kind of trousers during the early James Bond films.

They had a store on Piccadilly, which was called DAKS' Simpsons of Piccadilly. That store had curved glass fronts, designed so that shoppers could see the garments clearly without being obscured by any reflections. They were the first in the UK and the largest in the world at the time. They sold that store to Waterstones, relocated to Old Bond Street and dropped the 'Simpsons Piccadilly' from the brand title.

'How can I help you, Mr Franks?' I said, removing the last biscuit from the tower and gobbling it up.

'I'm interested in what you're doing. Especially in Asia. We want someone like you to be our new creative director at DAKS. What do you say?'

'Creative directors are all the rage right now, Mr Franks,' I said. It was true. Fashion houses had seen the likes of other creative directors like Tom Ford turn around the ailing fortunes of Gucci, and DAKS were on the lookout for the same injection of vitality.

'So, what do you say, Timothy?' Jeremy said, catching me off guard.

'I'm flattered. But you know, we're a small team here, and we're already very stretched. I've got my own business, not a nine to five, by any means – it's a way of life. I have just taken on a collaboration with Marks & Spencer, I've got Tom Cruise on the other line needing a suit for the Oscars and I'm knackered from doing all the Olympic uniforms. I'm not sure I have the headspace for anything else.'

There was a long pause. Uncomfortably long. Finally, 'Good. Good. I'll have my people send a car for you this weekend. I'll see you at the show, Timothy.'

'What show?'

'Bring a smart pair of Chelsea boots, just in case. You never know if and when the heavens will open, and all the hot dog stands are outside the hospitality tents.' He rang off.

Jeremy was referring to the Royal Windsor Horse Show and DAKS were one of the proud sponsors. The Royal Windsor Horse Show was first staged in 1943 to help raise funds for the war effort and hosts an assortment of international competitions in show jumping, dressage and so on.

Windsor Palace overlooks the main stadium, and one can't help but get swallowed up by the grandeur and pomposity of it all. In the DAKS hospitality tent, there was a live-lounge jazz band and plates of foie gras and canapés were being hoovered up by the snatching paws of hungry punters. Jeremy was in a huddle of immensely well-turned-out individuals, some in their morning coats, most in their traditional herringbone tweed Norfolk jackets in green and brown hues.

'Timothy, dear boy. You made it!' Jeremy cried, loud enough for the entire tent to hear.

No sooner was I greeted than a glass of Pol Roger champagne was thrust in my hand.

'This is Timothy,' Jeremy bellowed to the rest of the group, presenting me proudly like one of the queen's show ponies. 'Timothy is going to come work for us.' He slung an arm round my shoulder and squeezed.

I recoiled slightly, but not enough to embarrass him. 'Well, Jeremy, I haven't quite …'

'Marvellous!' came the chorus of agreement from Jeremy's friends.

'Yes, he's exactly the person we need for DAKS to take it forward,' said another, chinking my glass with his.

Catherine and I joined Jeremy and his friends for dinner in the marquee while the events of the day carried on around us. 'Tim, would you and Catherine care to join us in the Royal Box?' Jeremy asked and dabbed a drip of gravy away from his mouth with a monogrammed serviette.

'Sure,' I said, although I knew Jeremy had misspoken. We'd be seeing the royals enter the box from the sponsors' seats and not sitting in the Royal Box itself. Turns out, I underestimated Jeremy, and we were in fact being escorted *inside* the Royal Box.

Jeremy relaxed into his seat like one does when watching their children on sports day. Catherine pointed to the right where a small fleet of Range Rovers were nearing, and out popped several burly men in black suits – and a small woman in a Ferragamo scarf, wearing a quilted Barbour jacket. 'Oh fuck, that's the queen!' I said to myself.

The queen carefully entered the box, followed by the Duke of Edinburgh and several black suits. I was instructed by Jeremy to stand. The queen inspected her fellow attendees, did a double-take on me and, peering through her Silhouette frames, her mind read, 'Who the hell are you and what are you doing here?'

And that was that. I was swept off my feet in every sense of the word. At the end of the day, I thanked Jeremy and told him, 'I'm in'.

Later that week, Jeremy brought me in front of the board at DAKS and I asked them in plain speak, 'What do you want to do?' A gentleman in a dark flannel suit, which I hoped was substituting a much better suit that had been held up at the dry cleaners, spoke first. 'We really don't like the fact that the Japanese own us.'

'How did the Japanese come to own us?' I asked.

'We used to be DAKS Simpsons,' Jeremy said. 'It was a family business, a big dynasty from Hungary. Georgina Simpson's husband is Anthony Andrews, the famous actor. You might have seen him in TV shows like *Brideshead Revisited* and *Columbo*?'

I shrugged, 'Go on.' Although I was aching to talk about *Brideshead Revisited* because I bloody loved that show growing up.

Jeremy continued to weave stories about each member of the family. One member, in particular, stood out – Johnny Menzies.

'He's a waify, Karl Lagerfeld-looking chap,' Jeremy said. 'With a little ponytail, ex-Hungarian Secret Service. Had a nefarious streak. He owned two vintage Rolls-Royces, one of which he raced and won down at Pebble Beach. The other, he had Rolls-Royce build a machete into the door, in case …' Jeremy shrugged, 'Well, in case he needed it, I suppose. I knew his shoemaker down at John Lobb in St James. He told me, in confidence of course, that at his request, he built a small pistol into the heel of his boot.'

'That's so fucking cool,' I thought.

'He was a mischievous chap, and like most ex-Secret Service, there was something off about him.'

'How so?' I asked.

'Simpsons of Piccadilly used to have a lovely restaurant downstairs, before we sold the building. The business back then was run by Dr Simpson, a lovely old lady. Despite being Jewish, she had an absolute mania for pork and particularly crackling. Every Sunday, they had a roast of the day.

'Knowing this, the cousin would dine at the restaurant on a Thursday evening, order not one, but two Campbell's Bullshots, drink some very good expensive red wine and order up all the crackling; come Sunday, he would glean the utmost pleasure in seeing Mrs Simpson beside herself when the restaurateur had to explain that they were out of crackling again. Quite the ruse. He was something of a sadist in that regard, depriving a lovely old lady from her crackling, wouldn't you say?'

Jeremy smirked and thumbed his moustache. 'He put the business on the market. At the same time, the Japanese had just fallen out with Bernard Lacoste and needed another big company to fill the hole. In a panic, they bought DAKS as a sign of strength. Now, the Japanese, their speciality is licensing. They can license DAKS, sell DAKS, but they can't drive DAKS, and we're getting into a bit of a mess with it all, I'm afraid.'

'How so?' I prodded.

'Well, we lost a big contract manufacturing up in Larkhall. We signed a big deal with M&S to supply their trousers to keep the main factory going. Of course, M&S wriggled out, slippery buggers. Left us with a massive loss.'

'Can we save the factory?' I asked. 'Maybe we can do quick runs, short runs, some tailoring. We could do some premium collections, things like that?'

'We could look into that,' Jeremy nodded. 'This is your remit, Timothy. I'll have the board pull together the necessary numbers for you.'

Jeremy cleared his throat and collected himself. His next question was something he'd been meaning to ask me since our very first phone call. 'Would you consider reversing Timothy Everest into DAKS?' All the important words were enunciated so there could be no ambiguity.

Reversing one brand into another, or a reverse merger, is the acquisition of a public company by a private company so that the private company can bypass the lengthy and complex process of going public. Funnily enough, I had been thinking about doing something similar only a couple of months earlier. I'd noticed what Bernard Arnault was doing with Louis Vuitton. He was just announced as the world's richest man in fashion in 1999. Fast forward, and today he's richer than Elon Musk.

I pondered on the idea of an exclusively British consortium, stock-piled with all the undervalued businesses like Penhaligon's, Sunspel, John Smedley, Chester Barrie and Macintosh. There were several discussions with various people I considered key players but we could never quite get it together. Now, maybe, here was my chance.

'You're not one for small talk, are you, Jeremy?' I smiled.

'We know you're not here for the biscuits.'

'Not these ones I'm not,' I pointed towards a plate of miserable fig rolls. 'These look like they've been here longer than you have.' I was enjoying myself, and so was Jeremy. 'I'd be interested, but I'd need the full support of the board.'

'We'll support you as a board,' Jeremy confirmed, 'and when the time is right, we'll buy the company back off the Japanese and we'll reverse you in. Timothy Everest will be the Ralph Lauren of the portfolio.'

The board nodded as one.

They put me in an office just off Bond Street and gave me a swanky new car and an even swankier salary. I was offered a big 'Golden Hello' – a six-figure sum, which I never took. If things weren't going to work out, I didn't want to be obligated in any way. (In hindsight, that was one of my more stupid decisions. I should have signed, taken the money and left anyway.)

It proved to be very difficult running both the Timothy Everest business and having to come up with a new strategy for DAKS. The Japanese were also looking to streamline the board and close the factories. DAKS was making drastic cutbacks and I had the unenviable task of trying to appease the workers who'd just been laid off. Meanwhile, the Japanese board were getting countless millions from the licence and (as we found out later) were cooking the books. On top of that, their annual expense bill was over £2 million, which was utterly ridiculous.

Back in London, I was tearing my hair out trying to come up with a strategy for a business that was haemorrhaging cash. I got a phone call from Stephen Quinn, who was the publishing director for British *Vogue* – a man renowned for his negotiating abilities and penchant for red socks. 'I want to talk to you, boy!' he bellowed.

'Actually, Stephen, you were also on my list of names to call.'

'Want to drop the monthly spreads, do you?'

By monthly spreads, Stephen meant the rolling advertisements DAKS bankrolled for British *Vogue*. We had started to skip the odd month due to cutbacks and this didn't go unnoticed by Stephen. As part of the advertisement package, we also got editorial features and inclusions in various listicles.

'I ...'

'Look,' he said, cutting me off. 'I can't give you any editorial in *Vogue* if you don't advertise. It's just the rules of the game, my boy. But as a friend to Jeremy, and to you, just take out a page in September or February, or whatever. Just a couple a year to keep up appearances. Do that and I'll support you.'

'Thanks, Stephen. OK, let's run with ...'

'Look at what that Rose Marie Bravo is doing with Burberry,' Stephen ran over me again. 'They've been going for four years with Rose. She's overseen eight seasons as CEO. Eight! Seasons!' Stephen hammered each word as if he couldn't believe them himself. 'Look closely at what they're doing and try and piggyback off their success. Because in places like Japan, Burberry sits side by side with brands like DAKS, like Aquascutum and so on. Come up with something new. It's going to take you a few seasons to get back on track because right now, boy, DAKS is all over the road.'

Stephen was right. DAKS was not going to get fixed overnight, and the business I had inherited was broken at its core. The brand postured like a reigning king who never left his castle. His armies were spread far and wide, with licence to carry out the king's wishes, but had become dislocated and lawless. In other words, there was no brand identity. All the licensees in Japan, Taiwan, Thailand, Korea, all had carte blanche, with no one looking over their shoulder.

The first thing I put out was an idiot-proof pack for all the retailers. It contained enough flex, so it wasn't entirely regimented, and it didn't look like overreach. In the meantime, I had Jeremy calling me night and day, asking where my great idea was for DAKS. What was the hold up? Worse still, he would try and fly his own ideas past me.

'What about DAKS sports?' he said.

'We're not an athleisure brand, Jeremy.'

'DAKS denim. Let's do denim. Let's do it better than Levi's, better than ...'

'We're not doing denim. It's not our area, believe me.'

'Well, I suggest you decide upon what area we should occupy and dominate. And do it quickly, Timothy.'

I hung up. But I knew I was running out of time. Jeremy had been good to me, and had instilled a lot of faith, which can put added pressure on a man. I stopped returning Jeremy's calls. When he came by the office, I would duck out the back and hide in a nice little restaurant on Albemarle Street.

On one occasion I went there, I bumped into Tom Ford, who had his offices close by. I knew Tom to say hello to and nod and be polite. However, I was closer to his late husband, Richard. I remember once Richard called me for some advice on cars.

'Timothy, it's Richard Buckley.'

I sat up straight in my office chair, 'Hello Richard, what can I do for you?'

'Well, Tom and I have bought this ranch out in New Mexico. We want to buy a car to get around in. But you know how he is, always obsessed with the details.'

'That sounds like the Tom I know,' I said.

'Exactly,' Richard coughed, and took a moment to consider his next words carefully. 'Anyway, you know all about cars. At the moment, it's a coin toss between a vintage Jeep Cherokee or one of those new blacked-out Range Rovers. Which one do you think we should go for?'

'Well, Richard, the Range Rover would be a marvellous choice. But you'll be in the middle of dust country. You'll be constantly cleaning that thing, you'll never be able to keep it immaculate and that will drive you both around the bend, if you pardon the pun.'

'I think you're right, Tim,' Richard laughed.

'That said, while I would personally have the Jeep Cherokee, the Range Rover would suit Tom down to the ground.' In the end, they followed my advice. We were hardly on each other's Christmas card list, but I do miss Richard. He was an extremely intelligent man and oozed class.

Meanwhile, my great idea simply wasn't coming. Reluctantly, I took a call from Jeremy when I was out in Seoul. 'Timothy, where the blazes have you been? We need to have a plan of action to take this forward. What. Is. The. Plan?'

I was extremely jetlagged and completely bereft of any ideas on how to resuscitate this sunken, weary battleship of a brand. I spotted a road sign as I crossed a bridge. E1, it said, in white letters on a blue background, haloed perfectly by a pictogram of a bridge.

'Jeremy,' I said collecting myself. 'We will start a subsidiary of DAKS called 'DAKS E1'. E1 is very cool right now. As you know, my Timothy Everest studios are based out there. Think about it, E1 as a concept. It's illusory: it could mean everything and nothing all at once. This gives complete artistic licence to incorporate sports, denim.' I knew Jeremy loved the word denim. 'It can have a life of its own outside of the world of DAKS.'

It must have smacked of desperation. I was asked to engineer an escape plan for a multimillion-pound fashion empire and all I could muster was half a postcode I'd just seen on a road sign.

'E1?' Jeremy quizzed. 'Timothy, I think you're on to something. And naturally, you know "E-Wan" in Kansai dialect means 'the best'! The top of the tree.'

'Naturally,' I lied.

'Timothy, that's genius. Now call me when you get back to London; we're expanding the licence to Perugia.'

'Perugia? I wasn't aware there was any manufacturing in Perugia,' I said, giving the car in front a firm honk to signify the light is green.

'We want you to oversee it. I'll fax all the details through so you can make some calls while you're out there. Find out if these guys are on the level.'

When I got to the hotel, I phoned around a few people in the industry at some very unsociable hours and, as expected, got some very ordinary feedback on the Perugia deal. I called Jeremy back straight away.

'Jeremy, don't get into bed with these guys, they're not straight.' I laid out my misgivings, but somehow knew it was falling on deaf ears. The decision had already come from higher up and a few weeks later, I was sent to Italy to police the production. Sure enough, it was horrible. The quality of the fabric was so cheap and tacky it made raw calico look like sea island cotton.

It made me very unpopular with the Italian workforce and the Japanese board, but I sent everyone home and told them we were hitting pause until we figured it out. Back in London, I called Jeremy. 'This will torpedo the business. We can't put our names on this. It will ruin us. Think about those horrible kind of shirts you find in tourist only shops on Oxford Street or Las Ramblas – it's worse than that.'

'Fine,' Jeremy grunted. 'Make the changes. Whatever it takes, you're in charge.'

It was back to the drawing board for DAKS. It was a brand that was in dire need of a reality check, and you don't get any more real than the streets of Shoreditch. And it would feed in to the E1 theme that Jeremy and I had settled on.

We recruited two young male models and shot them playing tennis overlooking some council houses near Tower Hamlets. That campaign came out looking so good that despite DAKS having zero budget for marketing, the magazines had no choice but to run with it.

The next step was to fly to Florence and present the collection at Pitti Uomo. Pitti is also a chance for brands to flex their creative muscles, and there is always a battle of one-upmanship to have the coolest and most innovative display. For the marquee brands with deep pockets, the focus is more on the presentation and less about the clothes themselves.

We needed to create a buzz around DAKS at Pitti with an installation so memorable they'd name a pizza topping after it. I remember seeing Paul Smith and his first showing at Paris Fashion Week. At a time when most brands were going through the motions of throwing clothes on mannequins and inviting people in, Paul erected a row of seven stripped-pine doors, all of them nailed shut bar one. Behind the working door sat a pretty young girl with porcelain skin behind a French Louis XVI style desk that had a walnut finish and brass trims. On the desk sat a white rotary telephone. After several attempts the buyer would find the working door, and the young girl would book them an appointment to see the latest Paul Smith collection that was on display in the hotel around the corner. That is the genius of Paul Smith.

Riffing on that idea, I designed a beautiful white polished box, ornate with British racing stripes and centred with a MOD target in a DAKS check. The collection was only visible from the inside and was strewn on floating white tables that gave it an ethereal, otherworldly quality.

The reception was phenomenal. No one was more pleased than the Japanese director, Hideo Miki (*Shachō* Miki, '*Shachō*' meaning president), an elderly gentleman with grey hair but even greyer skin. 'Everest-san, fantastic! That's why you're creative director. Stroke of genius, Everest-san. Fantastic!'

'Thank you,' I said. 'It wasn't that difficult.'

'You come to Japan, Everest-san, with this.' He waved a cursory hand at the display. 'You talk to our buyers. You talk to our press. I want them to see the genius, this exhibition. But for our people.'

A week later, I was in Japan. My team were sent ahead to assemble the exhibition to my specifications, and they did it even better than the original. It was a riot, and once again, everyone was ecstatic. I must have shaken more hands than a politician at an assembly rally.

A young Japanese intern in bootcut selvedge was tugging at my arm every five minutes. 'Timothy, will you meet the photographer?'

'Alright, Bootcut,' I said, relenting finally. He was like a dog with a squeaky toy. There were some very important buyers that I needed to speak to and having my photo taken at this very moment was not a priority for me in the slightest. But I knew Bootcut wouldn't let it go. I was marched into a room where a dozen eager-faced kids had eddied around a large table. I sat down at the head and let Bootcut make the introductions.

'Timothy, this is Hero.'

Hero did a deep bow.

'Pleased to meet you, Hero,' I bowed ever so slightly. 'What do you do?'

'I'm a photographer,' Hero said, with a nervous smile.

'Oh, do you want to take my photograph now?'

'No, I take photographs.' Hero didn't elucidate, so I moved round the table.

Next to Hero was a young girl with soft features and brown hair in a classic bowl cut. 'Who are you?' I asked.

'I am photographer's assistant.'

'Don't tell me, you assist the photographer.'

'Yes, very much I assist him.' She laughed a very natural laugh. Everyone around the table was smiling receptively, yet I felt like I'd missed a memo for this meeting. And so I continued.

'Who are you?' I pointed at the only young man in the room wearing a shirt and tie.

'I am creative director,' he said.

'That's funny, I thought I was the creative director?' I said.

'No, I'm the creative director of the agency. We do all the advertising and marketing DAKS here in Japan.'

I was still none the wiser. Now I know what it must have felt like for people at that Paul Smith exhibit trying to open doors that were nailed shut.

'And you?' I asked the young girl next to him.

'I am creative director's assistant.'

Suddenly, the penny dropped. These kids weren't here to take my photograph. They were here to take my ideas. I stood up and sighed a long 'Ohhhkay', the way one does when they're fed up. 'I think I know what's happening now. You've got a separate budget for your campaign here in Japan, and you want to copy the one we did in London, but you need me to tell you how to do it.'

The creative director clapped his hands. 'Frankly speaking, Everest-san, yes.'

'I'm fucked,' I said, and walked out.

I knew that if the Japanese shot their own campaigns using our templates, it would leave us no budget to shoot our own. When I spoke to our board, they were happy to compromise and placate the Japanese because they were more interested in the next salary than upholding an ideology.

Still, I couldn't argue with the numbers. DAKS was off to a flying start, opening sixty-two shops within a season. Behind the scenes, however, the wheels were coming off because between all of my other projects I was spreading myself thinner than a watered-down pint of Fosters. The stress was starting to show, especially when I had my seasonal meetings with Shachō Miki at my London office in Old Bond Street.

Shachō Miki was notorious for not liking air conditioning and he would throw his weight around my office, demanding it be turned off. 'Shachō Miki, it's boiling in here,' I said, wafting my silk tie like a cartoon character. 'We have air conditioning for a reason.'

'Keep it off, Everest-san. I own building, not you.'

After thirty minutes of us locking horns over budgets and direction, I excused myself for a bathroom break. Outside in reception, I asked my PA to turn the air conditioning back on.

'Timothy, don't be so petty,' she pleaded.

'To hell with him, this is my office. Turn it back on.'

When I returned to the office, Shachō Miki gave me a look that was enough to chill any room. He rolled his shoulders and puffed his lips like a horse does when it's being shepherded to its stall. He muttered something to his assistant, who gave me the same icy stare and left the room. Sure enough, ten minutes later the room was cooking again.

And so, this pathetic dance played on between us throughout the afternoon. Every time someone from my team would go out and turn the air-con on, as soon as they returned, Shachō Miki would dispatch one of his team to turn it off.

Shachō Miki was as stubborn as a mule, and loved nothing more than having me write up weekly reports on what was going on with the business in London. 'Everest-san, where is my report?' he would bark over the phone.

'I don't have the time for this kind of bureaucratic overreach. The extra zeros I'm putting on your quarterlies is the only progress report you should be interested in.'

Still, the workload was catching up with me and something had to give. It all came to a head on my next visit to Japan, and I arrived at Shachō Miki's office, deliberately dressed down in a soft pale blue jacket, far too casual for the formalities of business. Shachō Miki picked up on it the minute I stepped through the door.

'Everest-san, why are you not wearing a suit?'

'It's good enough,' I said firmly, knowing it wasn't.

'You look like you're ready for golf.'

We exchanged a few more barbed comments, although it didn't get out of hand. No crockery was thrown around the room, but we both knew we were coming to a crossroads.

'Everest-san, the trouble with you, you think you own the company. You do not. I own the company.' It was an undeniable truth.

'Yes, that is a problem, isn't it?' I said smiling. We both had a little laugh and I agreed amicably that I would leave. They offered me to stay in a different capacity, but I said no. I couldn't continue if they couldn't support my vision to drive the business forward. Still, I bore no grudges especially, as they did compensate me very well when I left the company. I didn't take my 'golden hello', but I did leave with a 'golden handshake'.

15

David Beckham

'When I'm driving, I can forget I'm David Beckham.'

David Beckham, *GQ*

In 2000, I clocked up an impressive total of 120 flights, most of them long haul. Those, I didn't mind as much; the killers were the short flights to Europe, which meant getting the first out at an unconscionable hour and getting the last flight back. Some days, I wouldn't even see daylight. My girls would often tug on my trouser leg at the airport nearly as hard as they tugged on my heartstrings as they sobbed and pleaded with me not to go, although Catherine would later reassure me that it was mostly histrionics.

The one thing I learnt about being away so much was that when I returned home, I had to deliver on my promises. If I said I'd pick them up from school on Thursday, I picked them up from school on Thursday. If I promised to take them to the park, I took them to the park. All kids really want at that age is continuity.

We'd moved operations from Princelet Street to Elder Street and just had English fashion journalist Hamish Bowles write a very nice article about me in American *Vogue*. We had set up a shoot for the article on 'The New Bespoke Movement Coming to America' just outside our building. The cameraman had adopted an irksome Kubrick-style attitude, wanting a thousand different shots from a thousand different angles of me walking towards him while he was lying on the pavement. I managed to wrap it up by kicking the camera with my boot as I went past him.

'That was close,' he said, eyeballing me suspiciously. I remained stoic. 'Shall we call it a day then?'

'I think that would be for the best,' I said semi-sarcastically.

Off the back of that article, I got a call from an upcoming stylist by the name of Kenny Ho. He had just got the gig to dress David Beckham and Victoria Adams for their wedding.

Kenny brought David round to Elder Street for an initial fitting, and we touched upon the broad strokes of what a morning dress would look like, knowing we had to pivot greatly on Victoria's Vera Wang wedding dress.

I suggested an ivory frock coat that was just a little longer than your standard look. David loved that because he and Victoria would often be seen out with matching colours, a theme carried throughout the wedding as they wore matching violet outfits by Antonio Berardi for the reception. Those suits have been the subject of public ridicule ever since. Even David has joked about them on shows such as *The Late Show* with James Corden and *Desert Island Discs*, comparing himself to something out of the Jim Carrey movie *Dumb and Dumber*.

I found David to be a very modest individual, especially on the subject of his own popularity. He once asked for my advice about travelling to Japan as he was due to play an exhibition match out there. I gave him a list of restaurants he should visit, and I asked him how he got on when he came to see me a week later.

'I didn't realise how well known I was out there already. I got off the plane, was driven straight to the hotel and was greeted by an army of fans screaming for me. I couldn't leave the hotel because they had all camped outside. In the morning, I got on the team bus, played the game and then got driven straight to the airport. Still, it all looked very interesting from my hotel window.'

I got to see some of that media frenzy first-hand. Despite every discretion, word got out that David was seeing me to have his suit made and one morning I turned up to the shop with the paparazzi camped outside my doorstep. 'Where's David?' they yelled. 'When's David coming? What time is David arriving?'

'Look, I don't know who you're talking about,' I lied, burrowing my way through the stampede, though no one was interested in taking my photograph. I said to the mob over my shoulder, 'But if it's who I think it is, then you're too late. He's had his final fitting and we're not expecting him back.'

That part was the truth, but it didn't stop them from buzzing round the shop like starved wasps. 'How did they find out about David?' I pondered.

Later that week, I had a call from the CID of the Metropolitan Police informing me that I was on a list of several people whose phone had been hacked by the tabloid paper *News of the World*. This put me in a rather invidious position as the editor, Andy Coulson, and former royal editor, Clive Goodman, were good clients of mine and had spent quite a bit of money with me. I decided not to prosecute and no more was said.

16

And Action!

'Need I remind you, 007, that you have a licence to kill, not to break the traffic laws.'

Desmond Llewelyn as Q, *GoldenEye* (1995)

Mamma Mia!

In 2008, I was enlisted to work on the film *Mamma Mia!*, a jukebox musical comedy based on the 1999 ABBA musical of the same name. Colin Firth and Pierce Brosnan starred, and it was through Colin that I got the gig. I'd made for Colin the previous year, in the movie *The Accidental Husband*, where he starred alongside Uma Thurman. When you satisfy the needs of an actor or a client then you will always get recommended for the next job.

'Timothy,' Colin said, 'I appear to have a very problematic chest.'

'Why is that, Colin?' I asked.

'Well, no one, at least no one comprehensively, has managed to make a suit that can fit my chest without pulling or bowing.' Colin was throwing down the gauntlet.

I replied, 'I can see you have a broad chest and compared to others that I've made for over the years, it is rather low in proportion to the rest of your body. But there is no reason why any tailor worth his salt cannot make you a suit that will fit that chest. And I will prove it.'

And I did. I was very happy to restore his faith in tailoring with a grey three-piece suit; a wonderful suit.

I flew out to New York to meet with Ann Roth, one of the most legendary costume designers in the film-making industry. She's worked on countless films, TV and theatre productions and, to date, has two Oscars for her work on *The English Patient* and *Ma Rainey's Black Bottom*.

Ann was a delight, but sadly I cannot say the same for her assistant, who was of a similar age to me and was probably hoping for a more seasoned gentleman to match the calibre of her boss. At every turn in the conversation, she was eager to dismiss me, my ideas and my credentials.

Luckily, Ann took a shine to me, and in her proper way always insisted on calling me 'Mr Everest', despite me being not too far north of 40. At the end of the meeting, we had signed off on the ideas for dressing Colin in a dark three-piece suit. 'Mr Everest,' Ann said, 'as well as dressing Colin, would you consider dressing Pierce?'

'It would be my pleasure.'

'For Pierce,' Ann continued, 'we want something quite sleazy because that's his character.'

'That sounds like fun. We can put Pierce in a silver-grey suit, with some silk in there to give him a slippery shine.' Ann and I were really hitting it off, and she enjoyed our rapport nearly as much as I did, watching her miserable assistant sink deeper and deeper into her chair.

We got the measurements for both Pierce and Colin and reconvened at Pinewood where large parts of the film were to be shot. Ann greeted me with her usual effusive pleasantry. 'Mr Everest!' she called across the sound stage. 'Thank you so much for coming!'

'It's my pleasure, Ms Roth.'

'Can we start off with Colin?'

Colin was waiting in the wings. We fitted him and, to my relief, although not to my surprise, it fitted him perfectly.

He was cock-a-hoop and struck every pose possible in the mirror, as if he had suddenly leapt into somebody else's body and it was a marked improvement on his own. 'I told you he was good, Ann,' he said glowingly.

Colin was always very sweet. Every inch the English gentleman that he so often portrays in his films.

We had to interrupt Pierce's singing lesson when we did his fitting, and despite my best efforts to make him look reprehensible, he still looked imperious. He didn't give much away when he tried on the suit, but I got the impression he was happy because he asked if I'd consider making clothes for a film he was planning, the sequel to his 1999 incarnation of *The Thomas Crown Affair*.

It's funny how things connect. The original 1968 version that starred Steve McQueen in the titular role was one of the films that had a huge impact on me stylistically and I would often think about those beautiful Doug Hayward suits that McQueen wore so effortlessly when I was framing the Timothy Everest business in the 1990s.

'We're going to do it,' Pierce said. 'It's just a case of getting Rene [Russo] and I together and figuring out the schedule.'

The next day, I returned to set to deliver some suits and spoke to Pierce once more about the opportunity to make for him. This time round, he was a little less enthusiastic and the hum of whisky on his breath suggested he was a little worse for wear. Nevertheless, he was still one of the most charming men you could ever wish to meet.

After the fitting, Ann called me into the next room to get my opinion on some of Meryl Streep's jumpsuits. I was very humbled that my opinion carried any kind of currency with Ann's fantastic wardrobe team. Across the hall, I heard my name being bellowed. 'Tim!'

I looked out the doorway to see Pierce, stripped to the waist and wearing chocolate brown PVC flares, with tassels on each leg that ran from the knee to the heel. 'Not very James Bond, is it?' he said, laughing like a schoolboy.

Tinker, Tailor, Soldier, Spy

Through several degrees removed of friends, wives and neighbours, we were asked if Timothy Everest would come on board and make for Gary Oldman for *Tinker, Tailor, Soldier, Spy*. I was told Gary was being quite difficult with the wardrobe team, although I never got to see any of that personally. What people construe as difficult I normally view as 'challenging'. I think Gary likes to challenge people in their vocation, but more in an ironic way than in a literal sense.

Gary threw a bit of a hissy fit over some glasses his character was asked to wear. There was a dispute that the frames were not the right size for the proportion of his face.

'Look, I know what I look like on camera,' he said, making square shapes with his hands. 'If you've been acting for a long time, like I have, you know what the end result will be. And if we go with these,' he casually threw the glasses on the desk in front of him, 'I know it will look shit. I need different proportions.'

Gary wasn't being difficult, just direct. Which is sometimes what you need when working in costume. And he was right. He had been in front of the camera long enough to know what would work and what would look subpar. My colleague also hinted he was just being provocative to pass the time. After all, there is a lot of hanging around on set sometimes.

Soon after we agreed to make for Gary, the wardrobe team offloaded Benedict Cumberbatch and Colin Firth on to us as well. We used Elder Street as our main headquarters for all the fittings, which took several visits over the course of a couple of weeks.

While we had to breathe some nuance into each of the characters' suits, the brief was 1970s period style with a lean to an administrative look. We used traditional, functional tailoring, with a mind on what fashions of the time tailors would have been influenced by – bigger lapels, longer collars, wider ties, etc. The suits reflected the film's realistic, yet rather drab and pedestrian view of British espionage during that time, not the wham-bam bullet-dodging romps so often associated with spy thrillers. In lieu of any flamboyance or colour, we simply made them as textural as possible to give them some dimensionality.

We established a good relationship with Benedict and, through a stylist called Joe Woolfe, we were asked back to make for his wedding. Joe had a tailoring business on Percy Street, but his background was hospitality.

He was your typical 'hostess with the mostess' at the Metropolitan Bar on Park Lane, which the *Evening Standard* dubbed 'London's pre-eminent celebrity haunt of the nineties and noughties'. The likes of Patsy Kensit and Liam Gallagher would hang out there and many of its patrons would get recommended to us by Joe. You don't get to be head of hospitality at the Met Bar (although it's now a grill restaurant) without having a modicum of charm, and Joe had it in spades. Perhaps after seeing how much human traffic he was leveraging for us, he started up his own business as a stylist and took those high-profile customers of the Met Bar with him.

Back to Benedict. He was very sensitive about his wedding as he is a very private person. We made him a three-piece morning suit but there are no public pictures to be found due to the level of privacy attached to the ceremony. Benedict even had a drone expert to observe the grounds so no overhead shots could be leaked to the press. We included some personal details but they're not for public consumption. We also made another morning suit for his trip to Buckingham Palace when he collected his CBE.

Benedict is a very moral person. During our consultations he would show more concern about whether the wool for his suits was ethically sourced than the cut or the fit of the suits themselves. He once read an article while touring in Australia on sheep shearing and how it's common practice in some parts of the world for sheep shearers to cut off part of the skin around the backside of the sheep when they're young to stop the fur from growing there, and consequently prevent them from getting ticks later in life. It's an extremely cruel practice and will only be eradicated through greater awareness and more people taking a leaf out of Benedict's book and questioning their tailors on the provenance of their woollen fabrics.

Benedict was also in remarkable shape. We fitted him for his role as Sherlock Holmes and for his remarkable *Richard III* performance at the Barbican. Not only was he very lean, but incredibly strong. At the time we were making for him, he was in training for *Dr Strange* and was conscious of eating very healthily, which (I'm guessing) was one of the catalysts for him turning vegan. We even sourced silky bamboo fabrics to accommodate his beliefs, which came with its own challenges – but as tailors, we always rise to meet them.

Prometheus

For Ridley Scott's 2012 film *Prometheus*, I was asked to make for Guy Pearce, who was playing an elderly billionaire CEO. It was a Nehru suit made from a weird metallic fabric that the wardrobe team gave a dirty chalklike finish. It fitted Guy to a tee. Although later we discovered Guy was going to be playing a more elderly man and his character would walk with a slight hunch. We made some necessary adjustments to accommodate Guy's fragility, but for me, it soured the overall look of the suit.

Prometheus was set between 2089 and 2093. The mood boards on the walls in the wardrobe department were teeming with multiple references from science fiction comic books. I presumed these were all the magazines Ridley had read and absorbed when he was younger, and I found it fascinating how one could take inspiration from the iconography of one's past and use it as inspiration for wardrobe templates set far into the future.

Ridley was always very good at reinterpreting or predicting how the future might look. In 1982, he directed the arthouse blockbuster *Bladerunner*, which looked nothing like any other science fiction film of its time. It was dark and dank, with no shiny spaceships and aside from the flying cars, it was far removed from having anything super-futuristic. From the arcing neon signs to the weather-beaten trench coats, nothing was perfect, and everything looked like it had been upcycled at least once.

As a stylist, I've always had a good ear for trends, but I'm no futurist. Knowing what people might be wearing eighty years from now is a bit above my paygrade. Yet, I was happy to chip in now and then when the wardrobe and production design teams were brainstorming.

For example, one debate turned to eyewear. 'You can't have people wearing glasses in the future,' chimed a young chap from wardrobe, who ironically was wearing some tortoiseshell glasses that looked a little too effeminate for my liking.

'Why not?' I asked.

'Because you'd be genetically modified by then. You would be able to sort out all the human inefficiencies before they were born. Poor eyesight, alopecia, all these things will be a thing of the past.'

I placed my mug of green tea on the table, and in doing so, noticed some grubby lipstick marks around the rim. 'People will wear eyewear in the future,' I said. 'Even if they have the capability of looking directly into the sun without blinking. And they'll wear them for a whole host of different reasons.'

I made sure to slowly enunciate each word while scanning the room. 'Michael Caine, *The Ipcress File*. One of the most iconic actors in the history of cinema chose to wear Curry & Paxton glasses because he feared he would be overidentified with the character of Harry Palmer. He wore glasses so that he could remove them for other roles. Patrick Swayze wore glasses when he didn't have to because he wanted to be viewed as an intellectual. And as far as alopecia goes,' I turned directly to Tortoiseshell, 'Yul Brynner shaved his head because he knew it looked cool. You'll never stop people wearing glasses because we all know they look too damn cool.'

Skyfall

Jany Temime was brought in as the costume designer for *Skyfall*, and I took a shine to her straight away. She was very charming and glamorous in a way that seems exclusive to a certain generation of classic French ladies. She was quite direct, which is a crucial trait for someone in her position and mine. Tom Ford had continued his relationship with the franchise having taken over from Brioni in *Quantum of Solace* providing the suits for Daniel Craig. I was enlisted to make suits for Ralph Fiennes' character, Mallory, who would go on to replace Judi Dench as M. Judi Dench was, and still is, an institution within the James Bond franchise, so we had to establish him quite quickly as a man fit for one of the highest roles of administration.

It was important to the film's director, Sam Mendes, that Ralph could command the audience's attention for the limited time that he was on screen. We put various looks together. The double-breasted jacket was a very key part because they wanted Ralph to look ministerial, quite serious and someone that undeniably had the class and balance sheet to be a patron of Savile Row.

Dressing Ralph was fun and fairly frictionless, for the most part. There were the odd exceptions where Jany would ask me to put the seed of confidence in Ralph's mind. She wanted him to wear a deep sky-blue cotton poplin shirt and navy embroidered fleur-de-lis braces to support a pair of flat-fronted trousers that sat high on the waist.

'Don't you think this looks elegant?' Jany said to me.

'Yes, this is perfect and contrasts perfectly with Daniel's fashionably cut suits,' I replied.

'Good. Can you suggest that to him?' she said under her breath, even though we were alone. 'Because he's not listening to me today.'

I was familiar to this kind of 'thought-inception behaviour'. There are some days where my clients simply won't take anything on board and I will recruit my colleagues to plant the seeds of my ideas in their heads. Some days, it sounds better coming out of their mouths than my own.

It's not an enviable task being the tailor for a film because you've got to please absolutely everybody: the director, the talent, the designer and yourself. There's no point in making something that pleases everybody else but you, especially if it falls well below the levels of standard that you set for yourself.

I did get some feedback from the *Skyfall* project that pleased me. Jany and Sam were reviewing Ralph's suits next to Daniel's and, noticing the marked difference, Sam asked, 'Why does Ralph look more elegant than Daniel?'

On cue, Ralph unbuttoned the cuff of his bespoke suit and beamed, 'That's simple. Mine are bespoke.' In response, Daniel ran sheepishly back to his wardrobe team and asked his team if *his* suits were bespoke.

We continued to clothe Ralph for the premiere of *Skyfall* and we put him in a particularly good tuxedo that was of Savile Row length with deep shawl lapels and a cummerbund. Scottish fashion designer Patrick Grant later referred to Ralph's tuxedo as a great example of a Savile Row suit. Patrick is the director of bespoke Savile Row tailors Norton & Sons, and if you're not a customer, you might have seen him as one of the judges on the BBC television series *The Great British Sewing Bee*.

I don't think Patrick realised we had made Ralph's tuxedo, which makes the compliment all the more pleasing. Ralph was doing a lot of yoga at the time, which kept him in good shape and made my job of tailoring him much easier.

In contrast, Daniel Craig wore a midnight blue tuxedo for the premiere that was far more fitted than the one we made for Ralph. When I saw them side by side on the red carpet, I thought, 'Crumbs, Daniel looks like he is bursting out of his!' When someone is as muscular as Daniel was for that role, if you put them in something that covers them entirely it tends to make them look dumpy. Having something that is fitted is really the only option for someone of Daniel's physique, although one can always go too far on just how fitted one would like their suit to look.

Spectre

After *Skyfall*, both Jany Temime and I were recalled to make for Ralph again in the following James Bond film, *Spectre*. This time, Jany asked us to make for Dave Bautista, who played the henchman Mr Hinx, and Christoph Waltz, who played Blofeld.

We made a Nehru jacket for Christoph, which turned out to be a bit of a disaster, born of a catalogue of errors made by wardrobe. We got the measurements, and they sent on a picture that was transposed, which resulted in the jacket fastening on the wrong side. We alerted wardrobe to the issue, and they assured us this is what they wanted, so we delivered it.

Sure enough, when action was called on the first take of Christoph as Blofeld, he tried to fasten the jacket and immediately everything looked and felt very skew-whiff. Christoph was a bit nonplussed, but the wardrobe team were really pissed off.

My colleague, Lloyd, got a really stroppy phone call because it was panic stations for them. We sorted it all out in the end, but these things can happen when making costumes, especially when you're not in dialogue with the actor themselves. The Nehru jacket especially has been Blofeld's uniform throughout the franchise, so it was an important one to get right.

We had another set of dramas with the suits that we made for Dave Bautista. During a fight sequence with James Bond on a train, Mr Hinx is set alight and quickly removes his jacket before going up in flames entirely. Because Dave is very muscular, when he takes his jacket off it flips inside out, so the lining was just as important to get right.

We made a dozen skeleton suits for the stunt scene, much like we did for Tom Cruise and Jon Voight in *Mission Impossible*. The hero suits are for the close-ups, but during the fight scenes the suits get trashed, so the skeleton suits only have to mimic the shape of the hero suit.

I thought we'd done a stellar job on these suits because Dave was a huge hunk of a man. We fitted him in person, and he was an extremely nice chap. It's common when people are an unusual shape, such as Dave was; they are the most appreciative of things if you can make them look good – which we did.

So, it was quite a surprise to receive another distressing call from wardrobe late on the Thursday afternoon saying ten of the suits had a burnt orange lining, and two had a fluorescent orange lining. It might sound like a small oversight, but continuity is king in the world of costume.

This had to be resolved by the following morning, but our trimming supplier was closed for the day. I called up nearly every tailor in my little black book, and fortunately, we found one who had the exact burnt orange lining in stock. We managed to reline two of the jackets and, in a pinch, had them ready for Friday morning.

Our in-house alterations team were accustomed to working odd hours, and luckily for me, they were a passionate bunch; especially on a project like this when everyone could appreciate what was at stake. For their dedication, I'd always look to reward them well as a thank you. For example, during one of the Rolling Stones' sell-out tours, we were requested by Mick Jagger's production team to provide an alteration tailor offstage, just in case Mick needed something adjusted or repaired in an emergency. I found one of the girls in our team who I knew was infatuated with the band and was certainly capable of fixing anything in a bind. She sat offstage on standby, sewing machine at the ready, like a doctor with a defibrillator. She had one of the best seats in the house. She watched the concert three nights running and never even had to turn the sewing machine on.

A Last Word on Bond

It was very obvious to me that to grow the brand Timothy Everest, we'd need to increase our profile, and being associated with the James Bond franchise can really put your brand on the map. *Skyfall* and *Spectre* were great for PR, and it was an accumulation of these types of collaborations that was putting us on the kind of level that made marketing the brand a hell of a lot easier.

I had a hitlist of people we wanted to dress, specifically for the red carpets. Having done the Oscars already, I knew the publicity we could leverage having someone like Daniel Craig seen wearing Timothy Everest at the Grammys, the Oscars or the Baftas.

Annoyingly, my business partner at the time (and we'll get into some of that shortly) didn't understand the benefits of pursuing these associations. He couldn't understand that fostering these types of relationships was the very key to the future of our business.

The Man From U.N.C.L.E.

Costume designer Joanna Johnston called me at home one afternoon and asked if I'd ever heard of an actor called Henry Cavill.

'He's not on my radar, Joanna,' I said, and placed my Earl Grey tea on top of a classic car magazine that had a photo of a Granada Consort and beautiful red GT4 Ford Capri on the cover. On a small plate next to the magazine was a small piece of shortbread that I was saving for my elevenses.

Henry Cavill (I was told) had just wrapped filming on the new *Superman* movie, but he was not yet a household name. At least, not in my household. Joanna was putting together the wardrobe for a new Guy Ritchie film called *The Man from U.N.C.L.E.* in which Henry was cast as the lead, Napoleon Solo.

'Timothy, I need your help with this one,' Joanna said, cutting straight to the bones of the matter, which I always appreciated about her. I returned my shortbread back to its plastic housing and slid the tray back into the box, like a neatly filed document.

'I'm listening,' I said.

'We have a challenge on our hands with Henry,' Joanna continued.

'Don't tell me,' I said, cutting her off. 'He's massive. He is built like Superman. But Napoleon Solo does not cut the same frame as Clark Kent.'

'Correct, Tim. The difficulty is that Henry is going to be losing a lot of body mass for his new role. So, making for Henry, while he's losing weight, is going to be like shooting a moving target.'

'It's going to be harder than that, Joanna,' I said. 'There's a reason why the Incredible Hulk wears ripped clothes, you know.'

'We have a lifeline, though,' Joanna said optimistically. 'We have requested the ideal sizes that Henry needs to slim down to, and we have a mannequin built to those measurements. All you have to do is make a suit that will fit the mannequin, and in theory ...' Joanna trailed off.

To say I was cynical of this initiative would be quite the understatement. I had not heard of anything so incredible in all my time of tailoring.

'Well, Tim, as you know, everything comes down to time.' Joanna paused, and I grunted in agreement. 'We don't have a lot of time to put these looks together, so the mannequin will expedite the process.'

Sure enough, a few days later, I was sent a very lean but perfectly proportioned mannequin, complete with chiselled torso, enviable but not overly bulbous biceps and legs that looked like they were sculpted by Michelangelo himself.

Over the course of a few weeks, Joanna and I talked more about the style, the silhouettes, and what era of fashion we were trying to replicate for the principal cast. We settled on a glamorous 'Guards officer look', which was popular towards the end of the 1960s, despite the Guy Ritchie version being set in the early 1960s. It gave us more artistic licence with the colours and the fabric. Towards the end of the 1960s, people were wearing traditional things such as suits and military garb, but in a slightly more modern way. The checked suits we made for Henry were what I describe as a 'TV blue'. Moxon Huddersfield Ltd, which is a high-end British textile manufacturer of luxury worsted and woollen suiting fabrics, made the mohair for us, and it really popped on the big screen.

The cloth was an electric blue, embellished with a woven stripe through it. We retailored it a little from Guy's original brief. Guy was after a look closer to the period in which the film was set and closer still to what the original actors, Robert Vaughn and David McCallum, wore in *The Man From U.N.C.L.E.* series, which ran from 1964 to 1968. In the TV series, they wore cropped three-button Italian bum-freezers, much like the ones the Mafia wear in the opening scene of the original *The Italian Job*, where they push the Lamborghini Miura off the cliff face. Eventually, Guy was won over by what Joanna and I had put together for Henry.

When Henry came to us for a fitting, his physique wasn't just close to the mannequin they provided, it was identical – to the millimetre. He was on a high-protein diet, and he was only allowed small portions. I could tell he was a bit fatigued. Not grumpy, not rude, just a bit disconnected with it all. During the fitting, I got talking to Henry's trainer, Mark Twight from Salt Lake City. 'How did you get Henry into such good shape?' I asked, a carefully managed compliment to both of them, as Henry, although in the changing room, was still within earshot.

'Lots of exercise and diet obviously,' Mark said, 'but the most important thing people don't realise when training is sleep. You need to give your muscles the chance to recoup. A lot of people don't sleep enough, so they don't recover properly.'

He pulled out some photos from a burgundy leather satchel and showed us some examples of his previous films. He had trained the cast on the Zack Snyder film *300*. There were before and after shots of Gerard Butler and his transition over five weeks under Mark's regime.

During the first couple of weeks, the changes were almost imperceptible. Week three is when you really start to see some definition. Week four is radically different, but by the end of week five, their bodies are almost unrecognisable from week one. It was like Mark had showed me the simplest, yet most awe-inspiring card trick.

'How?' I managed to muster, although he had just told me how.

'It's just routine, Tim,' he said. 'Isn't that right, Henry?'

'Well, we'll be going to Japan soon,' Henry replied from behind the door. 'I can finally have some nice sashimi. And because it's good for you, I can eat as much as I like!'

Mark chuckled into my ear, 'He thinks that, but he'll only be allowed one piece.'

Mark showed me some more photos of his various clients. It didn't make me feel too good about my shape, I can tell you.

When I looked up from the photos, Henry was standing in the middle of the room in his Calvin Klein Y-fronts holding the dressing room door. 'What do you want me to do with this?' he asked softly, and we all burst out laughing. He placed it against the wall next to the dressing room and there it stayed until I sold the building many years later. When people asked why I didn't fix the dressing room door, I would always revel in telling them the story that Superman broke it.

Later, I was to discover through talking to Tom Chamberlin, editor at *The Rake*, that Henry didn't really enjoy wearing our suits in the film. This was understandable because the suits we made for him were quite fitted. Although Henry had lost some body mass, he was still very muscular, and he didn't need a suit to accentuate his chest or any padding to boost his shoulders. If I were making a suit for Henry to wear in his personal life, I would be suggesting making something with a softer construction.

But this is not uncommon. Actors will get an impression of our standards, good or bad, based on what we make for their character under the instructions of the director or the costume designer. We rarely get to have a conversation with the actor about what we would do differently for them personally.

17

Levi's

There is little benefit to the manufacturer to pay for storage space to keep an old concept model sitting around long after the vehicle has entered production.

Chad McQueen once said of his father, Steve McQueen, that he never once saw him look twice in the mirror before leaving the house. Throughout my career, I've often found the most stylish people are the ones who have more important things to think about in life than the clothes on their back. The same could be said for my old boss, Mike Hughes, in Wales, who used to wear a beaten denim overshirt whenever he went cray fishing.

Mike was a larger-than-life character, whose untamed blonde mop made him a cross between a young Jon Voight and a latter-day Boris Johnson. He would summer in Ibiza before it was trendy, and for some reason only known to Mike, he would always pretend to be German when on holiday.

His summer 'mufti' was a seafaring denim smock and white clogs. It's funny how these things stick with you and come to life in a different form later down the road. I used Mike's look as inspiration for when Levi's came knocking for a collaboration.

Levi's were looking to enlist a series of young designers and gave them each a nondescript length of denim and told them to create something in their own style. Most people made a pair of jeans with either some embellished stitching or superfluous press studs.

I thought it would be more interesting to tailor an overshirt instead, lifting some of the details from the 501s, so there would be a through-line. For this particular project, I teamed up with a chap called Mohsin Sajid, a student at St Martin's College and something of a denim professor. He currently owns a denim company called Endrime and is the kind of man who talks faster with his hands than he does with his mouth.

Together, we looked through the Levi's archives and stumbled across a story where Bing Crosby (a patron of Levi Strauss) was once turned away from checking into a Vancouver hotel for wearing a pair of jeans. Denim-clad clientele were apparently too low ball for this particular establishment.

After hearing this story, Levi Strauss and Co. created a denim tuxedo for Bing to wear, making him impervious to any kind of draconian dress codes on his travels. They even managed to get the president of the American Hotel Federation to sign off on the denim suit. It was a wonderful story to help promote the campaign but, truth be told, the Bing Crosby denim tuxedo, with its lurex facings and caricature frogmouth lapels, was quite ghastly.

Despite our collaboration being a commercial success, it was not the most satisfying of projects. I wanted to do something more tailored, but in the end, between the head of design and the in-house marketing teams at Levi's, we ended up with a reasonably nice compromise. A compromise similar to what lawyers would call a good divorce settlement, where no party feels like they won.

Levi's were keen to promote paper denim and hemp denim. The problem with hemp is that it stretches very easily and after one wear it loses its shape. To counter this, we made our version of a jean but with a sewed-in seam, like you'd have on a pair of trousers. With the shirt we would top stitch the pocket with the trademark Levi's accurate stitching, known as the batwing.

The white jacket we made was very heavily branded with Levi's insignias, but it was white on white stitching so remained extremely subtle. You'd only get to fully appreciate the intricacies if you were in the presence of someone wearing the jacket, and if you were looking for it.

Meanwhile, I had befriended a gentleman called Paddy, who was living in Japan. Paddy had this wild idea that shopping for clothes on the Internet was going to be the future of the industry. Yet Paddy still needed to create a physical space to show the product, although he'd only ever have one of each product in stock, which prevented him selling it there and then. People would see the product, feel it, try it on, then go home and buy it online and have it delivered.

The concept space launched on Savile Row and was a confluence of commercial innovation, such as sneakers stacked on tiered felt mats pressed against the shop window and rare products born of unorthodox collaborations. This is where we came in. We launched the collection in Paddy's shop and both critics and, more importantly, the customers lapped it up.

We were paid on commission and paid well, but crucially I learned a great deal from the initiative. We reached out to a much different audience and created some unique awareness for Timothy Everest, the brand.

Paddy was certainly onto something, but he was too early into the world of e-commerce by a couple of years and people weren't ready to buy clothes exclusively online. The infrastructure simply wasn't in place to cope with demands. For example, a customer would see a sneaker in the window in a size 9, like it, wish to make a purchase, only to be told they'd have to go home and order it online, then they'd receive the sneaker within forty-eight hours. Many people just went to Selfridges instead, having seen what they liked and knowing they could buy it right away. Paddy's shop ultimately had to close its doors.

Ironically, nowadays, when brands establish their business purely online, their plans for growth are to enter the physical space to show what they do.

The collaboration sparked enough interest for Dana Telsey to ask for me personally to tailor her for a suit. Dana worked for one of the big finance houses and showed all the character traits that I'd associate with an intense, dynamic Jewish lady. She was the expert in predicting fashion trends and if your name was on her lips, or in her column, overnight it would dramatically impact your share price, one way or the other.

Dana came with her husband for a fitting in my hotel room in New York. Her husband, in complete contrast to Dana, exuded an aura of complete relaxation. He dutifully unpacked the sandwiches he had no doubt made.

'You don't mind do you, Timothy?' asked Dana, biting into one of the sandwiches as she caught a small dollop of sauce in her napkin.

'Not at all,' I said, stretching the tape up her arm.

'It's the only time in the day where I'll have an opportunity to eat.'

Dana was often asked, 'What are the brands of the future?' In one interview, she kindly mentioned me and Richard James. This further cemented my reasoning for calling the business Timothy Everest. Other names in the hat were 'Pinstripes' and 'Flannels' (perhaps foreshadowing the name of my current business, Grey Flannel, which I'll come on to). However, successful brands like Ralph Lauren were living brands. That's what we were aspiring to, and that's what Dana had also latched onto. I was trying to elevate the brand by positioning it next to household-name brands. Much like Julian Dunkerton had done by positioning the unknown Superdry next to Cult Clothing and Bench, which were successful at the time.

With Timothy Everest, I always had half an eye on the next relationship. Sometimes, this bamboozled people on the outside looking in. They thought many of my seemingly off-the-wall collaborations were a waste of time, that we're tailors and should stick to our strengths, i.e., making suits. But I was playing the long game and was well aware of the potential benefits. If we were just making suits, we'd have nothing to sing about and no point of difference.

18

Jay-Z

Daimler announced that sales of all Maybach models and the brand would cease in 2013. Before the announcement, only 3,000 Maybach vehicles had been sold, with an estimated loss of €330,000 for each car sold.

Winter Park is a pretty dreadful, homogenised suburb of Orlando, devoid of any character and layered with rows upon rows of vanilla-looking buildings which I found impossible to distinguish. I had emigrated to Winter Park at the age of 19 with my friend Robert and this was how I described it to Robert's uncle when he pressed me for my opinion on the place. Only, I wish I hadn't been so forthcoming, because it turns out that my friend's uncle was the property developer who had created Winter Park.

Next to Robert's uncle's place was a strip club called the Booby Trap. The marquee entrance was bookended by two concrete domes that resembled cemented breasts, finished with two keystone wedges that looked like hardened but perfectly proportioned nipples. The Booby Trap was notorious to the locals as a den of crime.

On my first night in the Booby Trap, I was introduced to a lovely Jewish girl called Alicia. Alicia knew the garment industry back to front, having worked for both Tommy Hilfiger and Ralph Lauren. But more importantly for us teenage boys, Alicia knew how to have a good time.

Alicia went on to get a job working for Iconix International, which is a brand management company that had the licence for Rocawear, a clothing company founded by Roc-A-Fella Records, whose co-founders were Damon Dash and Shawn Carter, otherwise known as Jay-Z.

My interest in Winter Park and its not-so-many trappings lasted only two and a half weeks. I returned to the UK, leaving Robert behind, but stayed in touch with both him and Alicia – and it was a good job I did. Alicia called me in my office some years later.

'Hello Alicia,' I said, placing a hot cup of coffee between my thighs as it was particularly chilly in the office that day.

'Timothy, have you heard of Damon Dash?' she asked.

'No, should I have?'

'You should come to New York to meet Damon,' Alicia said. 'He's very prolific. Jay-Z fronts all the projects, but the success is largely down to Damon.' At that time, Damon had just financed a film called *The Woodsman*, which starred the actor Kevin Bacon, and he was in need of some suits for the press junkets.

I flew to New York that same week and ventured up to their office in Midtown for a sit-down meeting with Damon and Jay-Z. At the entrance to the building, a DHL man asked me to press the buzzer and keep my finger on it, which I duly did. He then rapped continuously for at least two minutes into the intercom, until he was near enough out of puff. Apparently, this was a daily occurrence, and not exclusive to DHL drivers either. I suppose if one fancies oneself as a recording artist and you have a direct line to the office of Jay-Z and Damon Dash, then one must make the most of that opportunity. I did feel bad for the DHL man, however, when the voice over the intercom instructed me to come up and to bring with me whatever the DHL man was delivering, if anything at all.

Once inside, Jay-Z was there to greet me and shake my hand, but no sooner had I been offered a seat than he was ushered away by his right-hand man, leaving Damon, Alicia and me in the office alone. And what an office. It was huge.

I sat in a leather chair facing all the ornately framed pictures of famous people that Damon had been photographed with. Everyone from President George W. Bush to Mandela was up there on that wall. I knew nothing about the world of hip-hop, but I was intrigued by Damon and Jay-Z because I was acutely aware these gentlemen came with an incredible loyal following who would spend a lot of money supporting them.

Damon informed me that his wife was Rachel Roy, a very established fashion designer in her own right, but he was more interested in talking about his current purchase, which was a 2005 Côte d'Azur blue Maybach with a cream-on-cream perforated leather interior. However, because Damon had a love for wearing vintage denim, the cream leather interiors had now been sullied with an ever so slight pale blue. So, he bought another one.

'But you betcha ass I won't be wearing denim in that motherfucker, Tim.'

'I hope not, Damon,' I replied. 'I can't imagine there's too many blue Maybachs in the US.'

'Fewer than a thousand. Still, at least I could get one, well, two now.' He laughed to himself. 'You rate the blue Maybach, Tim?'

I had to tread carefully here because the reputation of the Maybach was pretty average. In fact, it was common parlance in the auto trade that the Maybach were bought exclusively by rappers or others with new money and zero taste. When the Maybach was launched in the US, Daimler Chrysler invited rich rappers like Jay-Z to their launch.

'I'm always enamoured with any car that comes with a V12 engine,' I said noncommittally. 'And it comes with parking assist so the wife can also use it.' That was an unfair dig – my wife is a perfectly fine driver.

Damon switched gears in the conversation. 'You know what's out of reach for me, right now?'

'What's that?'

'Property on Star-fucking-Island. FL-OR-IDA. That is some serious "for real" estate up there, Timmy-boy. But those motherfuckers won't let me buy. The fucking neighbours, Tim. They be thinking I'll be partying all night, keeping their dull asses awake. Shit. Well, it might be true, but I'd invite those motherfuckers over for some ribs if they fuckin' let me in the fucker.'

'Well, it's a contradiction of terms, Damon. They can hardly call it Star Island, and with a straight face refuse you entry.'

'No shit.'

We both laughed. He offered me a Heineken, but it was only 10 a.m., so I turned it down.

Damon was very likeable, but I soon gathered he was not very professional about things. I can imagine that's why he hired Alicia. She was very proper and guided the conversations along in a productive way. Which ultimately bored Damon, so the meeting was cut short, and I left.

But Damon had seen enough in me to take a chance, and when he came to London, we dressed him. Damon and Jay-Z wanted me to do a take on the skinny Thom Browne look which was all the rage at the time. As our chats progressed, I convinced them that as larger gentlemen, it would make more sense to parody the matinee idol look.

'Why would you have one scoop of ice cream when you can have two,' I told them. I wanted to weave in some signatures that people would recognise from the Projects, a North American term for government-subsidised housing developments with relatively low rents. In the UK, we call it council housing.

I wanted to have Damon and Jay-Z looking elegant in a Savile Row style, but with subtle nods to the roots of hip-hop. We gave their jackets large lapels and went shopping for Homburg hats down at Lock & Co., the oldest shop in London.

When Damon came to London to promote *The Woodsman*, it was my job to ensure he was dressed properly for all the press junkets. There were a lot of costume changes involved with Damon, because he was not one to wear a suit if the cameras were not on him.

Damon had an entire entourage for his various interviews around London, and I suppose I was making up the numbers in that department. Studying Damon closely, I could appreciate first-hand that while he might not be the most conventional of businessmen, there is certainly something to be said for someone who has great instincts and can carry themselves with unbridled self-belief. After all, why would anyone doubt themselves, if they came from humble beginnings like Damon did, and went on to oversee a successful multimillion-pound record company, clothing company, film production company and so on?

At the newly built Soho Hotel, I prepared Damon for his interview with Jonathan Ross, which was happening in his suite with all the camera crew present. My job was done for the moment, so I relaxed in the lounge area of the suite with the rest of the troops.

Damon's troops were mainly kids, and they were all smoking a joint and handing it round. I hadn't smoked a spliff in years and on the rare occasion when I did partake, I was always prone to coughing fits. 'Just play it cool, Tim,' I thought. They handed me the joint, I puffed a couple of times, and started to recline slowly backwards on the sofa in the most refined way I possibly could. I leant back, further and further, until I was entirely horizontal on the chaise longue. My eyes became very heavy. 'Look it's the London Eye, boys,' I said, hopping to my feet and pointing out the window.

I asked my colleague after the interviews wrapped, 'Tom, did anyone notice my little faux pas back there in the hotel room?'

'You mean where you fell asleep after one toke on that joint?' he said, trying not to laugh.

I didn't see much more of Damon after the London tour. He was very professional when it came to paying me, but I got the impression he was overly spendthrift and quite reckless when it came to the company's finances, and it was only a matter of time before investors (who were mainly Russian) would stop supporting that kind of lifestyle.

Jay-Z, on the other hand, was becoming a household name and things were starting to take off for him big time. We met a couple of times when I was doing trunk shows in New York. I fitted him for a tuxedo, and we spoke about doing bigger projects together, but he went with Tom Ford in the end as Tom was the new face for menswear at the time.

However, it was a nice little interlude in my career, and I think on the surrealness of that time with great fondness. Some months later, I received a message from Damon on my answerphone. 'Tim, it's your boy Damon. I just want you to know. I was wearing your threads today, and Rachel said to me, "Boy, you look fly". Your boy Damon. Out.'

19

Rapha

Leith Hill is deemed to be *the* classic four-minute hill climb. It's the distance to suit riders with explosive power. One can train for these hill climbs all year, but when it comes to the race, one just needs that ability to push themselves into the red and hold it.

'Have you heard that racket out there?' asked Mum, as if the pilot light in her last nerve had just gone out.

'What racket is that?'

'Those kids on their motorbikes in the field, causing all that racket. Do you know them?'

'I'm afraid not,' I lied. I knew only too well who those kids were because I was one of them.

As a young boy, my mother never wanted me to ride a bike of any kind for fear of me getting into some kind of ill-fated scrape. Reluctantly, she agreed that if I was willing to work and save my own money, I could buy my own Puch racing bike. Puch is an Austrian company located in Graz, the birth town of Arnold Schwarzenegger, and was founded in 1899 by the industrialist Johann Puch.

They produce all manner of automobiles, and I was yearning to buy a motorbike so I could join my friends in the Motocross, a racing sport in which riders compete on off-road courses using motorbikes. However, my mother's blood pressure would never have been able to withstand the anxiety levels, so I had to start with the basics.

To make money, I worked the weekends of the winter months in the kitchen of my parents' restaurant, washing dishes for 50p an hour. Come summer, I toiled on the fruit farms picking strawberries and raking in a lucrative 26½p per tray, with each tray holding a capacity of ten punnets. The pay-out premiums would always vary depending on the time of season and how abundant the strawberries were. Some days it would sink to as low as 22p a tray, but you took those days on the chin, and I made sure to eat my fair share if I felt compensation was owed.

After many months, I had enough savings to buy my first Puch racing bike. Barring a few subtle differences, which were imperceptible to the layman, it was loosely based on the kind of road bikes one might see in the Tour de France.

Despite being immensely besotted with my Puch, I still couldn't push the thought of owning a motorbike from my mind. The novelty was rapidly eroding with each lacerating crosswind and the long clamber to the top of the Kentish hills would only herald a short, albeit thrilling white-knuckle ride to the bottom.

Inevitably, I upgraded to a two-stroke scooter and stashed it in a friend's shed so my mother could sleep soundly at night. It came with some minor defects. The throttle cable was broken so I jammed the fuel flow open with a matchstick, bump started it in second gear and used the kill switch as a brake. It had a hole in the exhaust which created a terrific din that rang out across the hills, and it was this racket that my mother was referring to.

Fast forward some years, when I was working at Malcolm's, a chap called Richard Clarke arrived at the shop on his push bike. 'What grown man chooses a push bike as his main mode of transportation?' I thought.

Richard was a romantic at heart, and soon assuaged my prejudices by speaking very eloquently about the unwritten etiquette of riding push bikes that every man who rides one should adhere to. Just then, and quite serendipitously, my reverie was broken by the arrival of two of our in-house marketing guys on Muddyfox mountain bikes.

'Strewth, did I miss a meeting?' I said. The boys looked at me, their shoulders didn't shrug, but their eyes did. 'What are these things?'

'They're mountain bikes, Tim,' one replied.

'Far be it for me to illustrate the obvious, boys, but last time I checked there are no mountains in London.'

'It's a new thing, Timothy,' the other one said. 'It's all the rage in California now, you know?'

'I didn't know,' I said. There was a time where you couldn't tell me a single thing I didn't already know about push bikes, but it only took twenty minutes for me to discover just how out of the loop I really was.

'Can I have a go?' I asked, hopping on, not waiting for permission. The Muddyfox mountain bike was a beast of a thing, and it came fully equipped with these revolutionary new things called gears – twenty-one of them in total.

Some years later, when I moved to Princelet Street, I bought a Kona mountain bike, a hard trail bike famous for its robustness. Not only did this bike save money on my commute, but it single-handedly renewed my love affair with cycling, and I'm pleased to say, my obsession with cycling to the workplace has stayed with me to this day. It wasn't always convenient to work up a sweat by cycling to work, so I'd flip between commuting on bikes and scooters, depending on whether I needed to lose any weight at the time.

In 1989, now in my late twenties but still in good nick, I took that Kona bike on a charity ride to Southend. I wouldn't say I gave the guys with their proper racing bikes a run for their money, but I kept them honest. After the race, the guys told me that I had them in stitches with my knobbly tyres whirring incessantly in their wake. But I did make it all the way down to Southend and I still have the t-shirt I was awarded for finishing.

Soon after, I decided it was time for an upgrade, so I bought a mountain bike from a gentleman called Robert Shackleton, who owned half of Princelet Street. My friend Jerry Aaron also bought one, and together we started getting very serious, importing parts from Santa Rosa in California to embroider our bikes. We developed a mania for it and, before we knew it, parts were turning up on a near daily basis. Anything from RockShox suspension systems, Manitou forks, Onza bar ends or Onza porcupine tyres – we couldn't get enough of it.

Jerry and I took our first big ride together down the Ridgeway, which was established as a trail in 1972, is the oldest road in the

UK and runs from the Avebury Stones in Wiltshire and finishes at Ivinghoe Beacon in Buckinghamshire. It's a beautiful but lumpy trail. Historically, pilgrims, farmers and soldiers have all embarked on the 87-mile hike, which stretches above and beyond the treeline. It's recommended that cyclists allow two or three days to complete the trail, but Jerry and I did it in one.

At the turn of the new millennium, more and more people were getting into road bikes, but just about anything on the sartorial side of cycling was pretty average. Mountain biking certainly had its look with its bright, Day-Glo, acid-house vibe. But if you were to wear that kind of clobber piling down Leith Hill and some poor old girl came round the corner, you'd frighten her to death. No one was catering to the casual commuter who was dead set on cycling to work but not keen on looking like they were in the middle of some kind of Iron Man competition.

Meanwhile, Jerry had really gotten the cycling bug. He folded his graphic design business, migrated to Bristol and opened a bike and café shop called Mud Dock.

Jerry was ahead of his time. He could see there was a groundswell of people who loved to ride bikes but loved the social aspect of riding bikes even more. Sadly, he was probably about ten years too early into that space, so sold more Mud Dock breakfasts than Muddyfox mountain bikes. But the food was (and still is) so good that it propped up the business and today serves as one of Bristol's most successful independent restaurants.

Jerry went on to manage a very cool mountain bike team that was sponsored by Volvo. 'I didn't pick the fastest riders, Tim,' I remember him telling me once over a beer. 'I picked the ones who looked the coolest. It's all about the aesthetics. The facial hair, the attitude, and how they can put all that together for the cameras.'

This conversation was scorched into memory, partly because Jerry was describing what Rapha went on to become. He envisaged a look, an ideology. 'Someone should look at black,' he said. 'No one's put together a look of black cycling clothes. If you don't do it soon, Timothy, I guess I'll have to.' This exchange had marinated in my mind for some time and came to the boil just nicely when the Rapha boys came calling.

Rapha is a cycling lifestyle brand founded in early 2004 by two gentlemen called Simon Mottram and Luke Scheybeler. Simon and Luke approached me with the idea of making a cycling suit.

'Do you know anything about cycling?' they asked across my desk one morning.

'I know a thing or two,' I said.

'We think road cycling can become really big,' Simon said. Of course, I'd heard all this ten years earlier out of Jerry's mouth.

'We already do some guerrilla marketing, but we're on a bit of a shoe-string budget,' Luke said, resting one elbow on his knee and his chin on his knuckles. It's a pose that someone makes when they're either bored or simply don't know what to do with their hands.

What Simon and Luke lacked in the way of a marketing budget, they soon made up for in creativity. They bought a Citroën van, unapologetically branded all the panels and doors with Rapha logos and lettering, and parked that monstrosity inside the Tour of Britain, the UK's most prestigious cycle race. They parked in all the quirky and awkward places they knew the camera would have to eventually pan to in order to establish a shot.

After our initial chat, they sent down their product developer, Simon Huntsman. Together, we fleshed out the initial sketches and ideas for the cycling jacket.

'How do you imagine this looking, Tim?' Simon asked, pencil in hand.

'I can tell you what we don't want this to look like,' I said. 'We don't want to end up making it look too period. As soon as this looks like something you'd see in *Oliver Twist*, it will lose all its coolness.'

Of course, despite me spelling out my apprehensions, it turned out looking like *Oliver Twist*. We made breeches and a short jacket with a high fastening. The sleeves were reminiscent of a fighter pilot's jacket, furnished with flaps that could be done or undone depending on the quality of the weather. The cycling cap had the low peak to make the ensemble more aerodynamic.

What set it apart was the fabric we developed with Holland & Sherry. It was a mottled grey three-piece with a nano-treatment which was not only quite modern at the time but made it showerproof. The crowning moment was seeing all the reactions to the promotional videos, where we threw bucket after bucket of water onto the suits. People would watch in awe as water rolled off the sleeves like mercury.

We launched the cycling suit with an elaborate installation in a pop-up in Clerkenwell and got an awful lot of press from that. We made a ready-to-wear version, limited to 1,000 pieces, which sold out fairly rapidly, except for the extremely large sizes, which was to be expected. On the back of that success, we became quickly known as the tailor to the cyclists.

One day, a senior barrister to the British Crown came into the shop and asked for something he could cycle to court in. We made him a suit for work then a suit to cycle to the pub in, once he'd finished with his judicial duties. We called it his drunk suit, presumably one he didn't mind getting the odd tear in when he inevitably fell off his bike after a night on the sauce.

As with most things, collaborations are never really lobbied for or targeted in a commercial sense. They are mostly born of conversations and happenstance and only become a success if there is enough passion to drive it on at every stage of the process. We can all be passionate when it comes to scribbling ideas on beermats over a liquid lunch, but it needs to go a lot further than that.

Simon called me some months into our relationship. 'Timothy, you have a minute?' he asked.

'I've got lots of minutes for you, Simon,' I said.

'I'm thinking we've reached a crossroads with Rapha. We're not sure what to do with it directionally.' Simon went on to explain his predicament and I could see he was in something of a quandary.

At the time, there was a huge renaissance with heritage brands, and everyone had become obsessed with vintage and tweed once more. The market, Simon and Luke's market, was becoming very saturated. The Tweed Run (an annual group bicycle ride through London where cyclists are encouraged to wear traditional cycling attire and ride vintage cycles) had become a parody of the very thing we were trying to sell.

'It's a bit like trying to convince customers that we are the original outfit, and everything else is just fancy dress. After all, how does James Bond repeat the James Bond formula after the success of Austin Powers?'

Simon finished spelling out his concerns as I finished off a slice of toast covered in sour cherry jam from the National Trust – pound for pound, the best jam in the world.

'If I may offer a piece of advice, Simon,' I said. 'I think you're worrying about the wrong things. You should be promoting the fact that the Rapha suits are all about movement, performance and practicality. If you have any reservations about the cosmetics, then strip it down to its cleanest form. You mentioned James Bond. When Cubby Broccoli handed down the reins to his daughter Barbara and his son-in-law Michael, he told them, "Whenever in doubt, go back to Fleming." Do you understand my point, Simon? No thrills, nothing extraneous. Just go back to your own source material.'

There was a pause on the other end, and in this moment, I realised I'd done everything I could to talk myself out of a gig. Tailoring was our handwriting. Stripping everything back to the essentials? Well, who needs a tailor for that?

'Thanks, Tim,' Simon said, and rang off. And that was me out of a gig.

20

MBE

After winning Le Mans in 1967, Dan Gurney took to the podium and received his magnum of victory champagne. He placed his thumb over the open bottle, shook it and intentionally sprayed the onlookers, thus champagne spraying was born.

As a shopkeeper, when a customer walks into your store carrying one of your branded shopping bags, it can only mean one thing – refunds.

Refunds are just a part of doing business, but some days it can really make you ache for a bottle of Teacher's. That Friday, it must have been National Refund Day, because I'd never seen so much money go out of the till in a single day.

Accepting defeat, I packed up early, and was hurtling down Welbeck Street on my pushbike when Catherine called me. 'Tim, I've got this really funny note come through the door,' she said, almost stumbling on the funny part. 'I'm not sure if it's for real, but they're offering you an honour. Would you like to accept an MBE?'

The Most Excellent Order of the British Empire is a British order of chivalry set up in 1917 by King George V, which rewards contributions to the arts and sciences, work with charitable and welfare organisations, and public service outside the civil service. There is a rank when it comes to the classes of appointments, but the ones people are most familiar with starting from the highest to the lowest are:

CBE – Commander of the Most Excellent Order of the British Empire.
OBE – Officer of the Most Excellent Order of the British Empire.
MBE – Member of the Most Excellent Order of the British Empire.

The royal family is an institution that is very dear to my heart. I grew up in a post-Commonwealth hangover, with a bankrupt nation clinging on to the embers and nostalgia of the Victorian Empire. But the queen, who was anointed just seven years after the war ended, was a beacon of hope for Britain, and gave our great nation some much-needed identity over her seventy years of service.

My first royal encounter was in 1969 when Prince Charles (now King Charles) came to Caernarfon Castle for his investiture. As luck would have it, that weekend we were visiting my auntie who had a house on the hill in Haven West. We'd gotten word the royals were going to drive past so we camped on the roadside with our little Union Jacks and caught the motorcades as they drove by.

My fascination carried through to my teenage years. Quite often, when the royals came to Wales, they'd moor off Milford Haven down the west coast. I'd zoom down on my bike and camp out there for hours in the thin hope I might catch a glimpse of them on the back of the Royal Yacht *Britannia*. I never did.

Some years later, Prince Charles came to Haverfordwest with Diana on his post-wedding tour of the UK. That's when I first saw Diana, who was the same age as me, or maybe a few months younger. I stood behind the railings on a typically drizzly day outside St Davids Cathedral. She wore a light brown suede beret and a belted trench coat with gathers at the shoulders and seemed to struggle with her umbrella as she juggled with the flower bouquets given to her by hordes of onlookers. 'Shouldn't someone be holding her umbrella for her?' I thought. Remarkable, though – what a difficult role for so young a person to take on.

These royal visits to Wales became the founding blocks for my patriotism. It does get under my skin a little when people talk about abolishing the royal family. The queen, especially, had that special connection with millions of people around the world. They talk about soft power, well she had it in spades. What they have offered us historically as a country is unique and sets us apart from other nations.

Normally, one receives an honour in their late fifties or early sixties. Unless you're a young, high-profile sports person who has achieved
something truly exceptional – the entire Ashes test-winning side of
2005, for example, or the Lionesses beating Germany in the final of the
European Cup at Wembley in 2023. (Although, incongruently, only
the captain, Leah Williamson and the lead goal scorer, Beth Mead, were
given honours, which felt a little mean.)

I knew perfectly well what an MBE was, and what it meant. Better
still, I knew that this was a wind-up, one that I was simply not in the
mood for.

'You what?' I barked at Catherine, coming to an abrupt stop outside
the back of Selfridges.

'It looks like it's been photocopied; it doesn't look very real,' she said.

'Oh, for fuck's sake!' I said, kicking at an empty Coke can on the street
and missing. At that moment, an elderly lady pushing a Yorkshire terrier
in a vintage doll's push chair, with several other terriers in tow, passed
me and scowled. The terrier in the pushchair scowled too.

'Sorry,' I said to her. I cupped the phone and said, 'Catherine, I've had
an absolute dog of a day at the shop. The kind of day that puts years on
a man. Whoever sent that note is clearly taking the piss, and it's the last
thing I want to be dealing with right now.'

'Well, I'm not saying it's not real, it just looks very, well, unreal. In
more ways than one, I suppose.'

'Is there a contact number on the letter?' I asked.

'Yes,' Catherine said.

'Do me a favour, give the number a call. Tell them you're my PA, and
you're just checking on it.'

Catherine did as instructed. I got back on my bike and was just making
my way round the back of Marks & Spencer, veering onto Granville
Place when my phone rang again. I leant my bike up against an iron
railing and picked up.

'It's for real,' Catherine said.

'Oh,' I said. 'I guess we better accept it then.' And we both burst
out laughing.

It was Gordon Brown who put my name forward for an MBE. I knew
Gordon quite well. My first time fitting him at No. 10 Downing Street

was the day he was signing off his first Budget as Chancellor of the Exchequer. Gordon was living in No. 10, and Tony Blair was living next door at No. 11 because Tony had a family and No. 11 had more square footage.

Gordon's office was a complete shambles. I didn't even know where to put my mug of tea among all the unindexed papers that were strewn across his desk. It was tea served in a neutral white, featureless mug. The sort of nondescript mugs that you get at large administrative board meetings.

'What do you think of the economy, Timothy?' Gordon asked, taking a quick slurp of his.

'Well, Mr Brown, I can only talk from the perspective of a small business owner. I think you've done a grand job so far resisting adopting the Euro. That's dicey waters there and I don't think we need gamble away our advantage for the sake of giving the Europeans a leg up. You've done well also dropping corporation tax for small businesses. A 5 per cent fall is the number I read about in the papers, so I owe you a pint for that.'

'Not at all,' Gordon replied with a surprised nod.

'But if you don't mind me saying, Mr Brown, I think it would be prudent to keep the UK gold reserves under the mattress for now, you never know when that might come in handy.'

After we sunk our tea, Gordon showed me his wardrobe, taking great pride in pulling out various jackets he had bought from Bergdorf Goodman in New York. He had a twinkle in his eye, did Gordon, but I don't think the public got to see that on camera. You don't necessarily associate Gordon with being an upbeat, jolly person to be around, but he was just that.

He was fascinated with clothes, and we neatened him up with many bespoke suits both as chancellor and as prime minister. Apparently, this was to the envy of Tony Blair, who would often ask Gordon who made for him, to which Gordon always replied, 'I'm not telling you'.

We also had the gig of styling William Hague when he was leader of the Conservative Party during that time at his office at the back of Westminster Abbey. It was quite surreal, on any given day, I could be privy to any inside intelligence overheard in Downing Street and vice versa, whatever murmurings would be coming out of the Conservative

Central Office. It had the makings of a very dry John le Carré novel – the tailor is a double agent, and he is doing more than sewing patch pockets to pinstriped suits; he is sowing the seeds of doubt in the minds of the most powerful men in government. Or something of that nature.

William was a tricky one because he just didn't do casual well. He also cut the kind of figure and profile that was hard to flatter. We'd tailored for him and just smartened him up. John Morgan from *GQ* put this powder on his bald head so he wouldn't look as shiny in photos – silly really, but you have to try these things. We did receive one great compliment from the *Telegraph* that said, 'There's been a change in William Hague, but we're not quite sure what it is.' It certainly wasn't the baseball caps that he wore on that famous photoshoot down a log flume as part of his 'Listening to Britain' campaign. We had no part in that, thankfully.

We made for David Cameron as well. Ironically, we made for more people from the Conservative Party and yet it was Gordon Brown from the Labour Party who put my name forward and signed me off for an honour.

They were to announce the honours list on New Year's Day, which meant Catherine and I were sworn to secrecy for the best part of six months. Once 1 January rolled round, my phone went off like a category F4 firework over London Bridge on New Year's Eve. Paul Smith wrote to me saying, 'Welcome to the club'. Mum showed me clippings from the village papers that spoke of the local boy done good, and my stepfather called everyone he knew to gloat about the news in case they hadn't read the local papers. He called me in a fit of euphoria, 'You bloody well deserve it, boy,' he said.

My stepfather was a fourth generation local businessman on the west coast of Wales and a farmer before he joined the army, working his way up the ranks to become a colonel by the time he left. He became the Mayor of Haverfordwest and even hosted the queen several times when she came to visit on her royal tours of the UK. He would tell me they had quite a laugh and a unique bond because they were of a similar age and shared a remarkable amount of life experience and responsibilities at such a young age. He also received an MBE but not until he was well into his sixties.

The truth is no one deserves one. You're just very lucky to get it. I was very flattered, but moreover, I was so pleased to share this honour with my team who had been with me from the beginning. It's extremely difficult to get a business going from the ground up and to follow through on a vision when others are completely blind to your ideas. We had this vision to bring some glory back to British tailoring and save manufacturing in the UK, like we did with DAKS and temporarily for Marks & Spencer until margin became more important.

As a business, we employed and inspired a lot of people over the years. There are plenty of derivatives of our business and I know of lots of people in the industry who were looking for Timothy Everest to take the lead.

One time, a young chap in the trade came into the shop and told me that I sounded just like his boss.

'Who is your boss?' I asked.

'Nick Hart,' he replied, 'of Spencer Hart.'

'Oh no,' I corrected him. 'Nick was under my wing at one time, so it's *he* that sounds like *me*.' Although, if Nick sounded like me at all, then he was just repeating some of the same phraseology that I would have lifted from Tommy or Malcolm all those years ago.

At Buckingham Palace, Getting Honoured

The year I received my honour was the first year that the honours were split between Princess Anne, Prince Charles and the queen. For the occasion I had made a new midnight blue morning suit jacket, remodelled my ivory silk waistcoat from my wedding and donned my sponge black and white trousers. I wore a stiff wing-collar shirt from Budd with a nice silk woven tie and silk lilac handkerchief. It was a very purposeful modern take on an Edwardian look.

They send you a little sticker to put on the car, and I drove Catherine's car, with my daughters in the back, down to Buckingham Palace. There have been many extensions and rebuilds of Buckingham Palace over the years, and I'll spare you the history lesson, but you have to drive through the courtyard to get to what's called 'the real Buckingham Palace'.

We parked up on the gravel and made our way to the red carpet. Inside, we went up some stairs where Catherine and the girls were syphoned off to one room and I was guided into another room where you've never seen such a nervous body of smart men and women anxiously shuffling their best shoes and fixing their hair in the reflections of light fittings.

The groups were then split up again and I was very pleased to learn that my group was going to receive our honours from the queen. Ahead of me in the queue were Rick Parfitt and Francis Rossi, the lead guitarists from Status Quo. Francis, in his chalk stripe suit and his red geometric tie, was twitching and bobbing up and down on his toes like he was about to compete in the 100m sprint. He and Rick kept doing relays back and forth to the toilet every ten minutes – quite understandable, yet quite the spectacle. Rossi later gave one of my favourite interviews to the *Guardian* about receiving the award:

> I'm not sure that we deserve it, but fuck it, I'm so made up it's ridicu- lous. You hear about people refusing them because it's not rock 'n' roll but that's a dickhead approach. My partner [Parfitt] is even more excited about it – he's probably blubbing. You start off rebellious, a teenager in a band, but you end up being part of the establishment.

Behind me was Jenson Button, who had just won the Formula One World Championship the year before. He wore a two-button mid-blue suit and I noticed he had made the schoolboy error of fastening both buttons. It shows a slight immaturity, fastening the bottom one of a two-button suit, but now wasn't the time or place to school Jenson, who still looked very smart.

A door opened and in walked an ex-army officer in full military garb with impeccable posture. He gave us the rundown on how the day was going to work and certain implacable rules to adhere to when meeting the queen. 'You do not shake Her Majesty's hand, until she offers hers,' he said, with great enunciation.

I looked at Francis Rossi and he was now bobbing on both his toes and his heels. 'He will wear those shoes out just standing,' I thought.

'Her Majesty is on a dais,' the officer continued. 'Which is a raised platform. Do not step on the dais.'

We all nodded in unison and were all very thankful that the instructions were not only clear but very easy to follow.

'Do not shake Her Majesty's hand and pull her off the dais.'

All our heads nodded again in perfect obedient synchronicity.

'That was a joke,' the officer said, in a far more casual tone, to which we all expelled a laugh that undid many knots from our stomachs. In turn, everyone was given a special pin to wear so that their insignia could be easily hooked on to their clothing when the honour was awarded.

One thing you learn from receiving an honour is how much pleasure the queen gleaned from giving them to civilians. The Commonwealth was very important to her: she devoted a life of service to promoting and protecting it. Her giving an honour to someone was a recognition of her appreciation for someone else doing comparable, albeit much smaller, duties. She relished the opportunity to meet and speak to people from all walks of life.

I was one of the very last to go in, and from the back of the room spied the queen on her dais with a small throne behind her. Catherine and the kids gave me a very proud wink and a smile as I passed them on the way. The queue ran serpentine all around the ballroom and the queen spent at least one or two minutes talking and shaking hands with each recipient. The orchestra played out Rick and Francis to 'Rockin' All Over the World', and they were smiling and nudging each other like they'd just cleaned out a casino. The lord-in-waiting called out my name from the register and gave the clipboard a firm tick with his pen. The queen smiled as I approached and bowed. I waited for her to present her hand before shaking it softly as instructed by the officer.

The whole operation was organised and orchestrated like clockwork. The queen clipped the insignia onto my lapel pin without any fuss or mishap.

'Congratulations,' she said, smiling.

'Thank you, Ma'am,' I said softly.

'How does it feel?' she asked.

'Well, Ma'am, I feel very lucky. I could never imagine when I started out in a small seaside town in west coast Wales that my clothing business would take me all the way around the world and bring me back here right now for this very humbling occasion.'

'Clothing business?' she said. Her eyes glimmered. 'Do you have shops?'

In truth the rest of the conversation is something of a blur. We spoke about my uncle in Wales, my stepfather having received an honour and the work that I had done for DAKS, which had led to us already crossing paths. Catherine told me afterwards that she spoke to me longer than any of the other recipients.

As I trailed away the orchestra in the balcony played 'Goodbye Yellow Brick Road'. Outside in the Quadrangle, they unhooked my medal from the pin and laid it carefully down in a Royal Mint box for me to take away.

Once back in central London, I asked Jeremy King, owner of the Wolseley, to put some tables together for myself, the girls and the staff. When we arrived, I got a round of applause and a glass of champagne from Jeremy, who has an honour himself but never talks about it.

When I look back through the photos that Catherine and the girls took of me that day, I'm smiling vacantly in every one. No doubt, I was more consumed with what was going on back in the shop and what had to be done. It's hard to live in the present some days, especially in days as surreal as those.

I've only worn my medal on extremely rare, black- or white-tie occasions, and often on the inside of my jacket as I prefer to be discreet about such things. I did wear my medal to Chelsea Arts Club on the day of the queen's funeral. We mourned, celebrated, toasted and over the course of a long afternoon consumed far too much alcohol. Only when we left the club did I realise, in a white-hot panic, that my medal was not on my personage.

'Oh, shit the bed!' I shouted, curtailing everyone's laughter and feverishly unfurling all my pockets. 'I've gone and left my medal back in the club. Lloyd, you're going to have to go in and get it for me,' I said.

'Why me?' Lloyd said, sobering up at the thought.

'I can't go back in there, Lloyd. I'm too pissed. Go in there and ask if anyone has seen my MBE.'

My friends folded in laughter. It's possibly the most ridiculous thing to ask of anyone. I can only imagine how foolish they'd sound to the barman, or the person in charge of lost property. Sure, a wallet, a phone, a set of car keys – all common accessories one can often leave behind – but an MBE?

Fortunately, Lloyd pulled through, finding my MBE unmolested in its little Royal Mint box, on the same picnic table where we were sitting.

'Here you go, "Sir",' Lloyd said, with a smirk, handing me back my medal. I've learnt not to take the medal out with me on any more Jolly Boys' outings since.

Some people do refer to me as *Sir* Timothy Everest, especially Americans. I never quite know what to do with myself when I'm addressed as 'Sir'. I normally just say thank you and immediately strike up a conversation about something equally as trivial. Some people are more comfortable with it, while others I know have turned down being awarded the honour altogether. A friend and client of mine turned down a peerage to save being beaten up in the press.

Another friend told me on a charity bike ride that he turned down one as well. This person is very anti-Establishment, anti-monarchy and went on quite the rant about how the honours system is too archaic and they should abolish the whole thing altogether. I bit my tongue. Sometimes you just want to enjoy a bike ride in the sun and not have to get into such matters.

21

Julian & James & Goatee

The most common remark made on a Morgan three-wheeler is that you need two hands on the wheel at all times.

Bread and Butter was a trade fair run twice a year by a guy called Karl-Heinz Müller, who had a store called 14oz in Berlin, which was reportedly the coolest menswear shop in all of Europe, if not the world. Bread and Butter was hosted in an abandoned airport, Berlin-Tempelhof, and its hangar was shaped in a semi-circle, 2km long, replete with retro fonts and a canopy-style roof that was big enough to accommodate contemporary airliners. This awning, the biggest in the world pre-Second World War, would provide shelter from the elements for both planes and passengers until someone designed the moveable tunnel.

It was quite bedazzling and there was a real fever of excitement surrounding the shows. Unfortunately, it went spectacularly bust but we always had a good time exhibiting there. That year (2011), I was there exhibiting a project that I had worked on with Brooks England, a cycling accessory manufacturing company that specialises in stylish leather saddles. I was manning my stand, sheathed in a black cashmere coat, black shirt, black scarf and black knitwear, when up waltzes a gentleman called Roger Wade. Roger was very industrious and entrepreneurial and had a collection called Boxfresh. He sold that at quite a young age to Pentland and years later, went on to found Boxpark, a food and retail park made out of refitted shipping containers. When it launched in 2011, it was described as the world's first pop-up mall. He has quite a few scattered around London now.

'Timothy,' he pounced, with a mile-wide smile and shook my hand. We exchanged pleasantries. 'Why are you wearing all black?' he asked, looking me up and down as if I had come dressed as Bananaman to a Spiderman fancy dress party.

'Because I wanted to,' I said, taken aback.

'Well, come with me. I want to introduce you to the Superdry team.'

'Why?' I asked.

'Because I think it would be a capital idea for you and the Superdry boys to collaborate on a theme around "bespoke casual".' Roger framed the words with his hands as if they deserved to have a show at the London Palladium.

'Roger, that's a ridiculous idea. It doesn't make any sense at all. Plus, I'm really busy here.'

'Just come over and say hello to Julian and James,' he pleaded.

I relented and met with the co-founders, Julian and James, in a secluded chat room that felt like it was purpose-built for mops, buckets and odds and sods. I was informed there was a third party to Superdry, a chap called Goatee.

Goatee had made a success for himself by launching a shop in Covent Garden called High Jinks, which had been selling extremely high-end skatewear brands and very exclusive sneakers. Julian wanted to add footwear to his portfolio and approached Goatee for some consultancy. Goatee wanted a larger slice of the pie, so Julian gave him some equity in this brand that wasn't worth anything called Superdry. But I'll get on to Goatee later.

Both Julian and James were courteous and polite, yet slightly guarded. It felt like a blind date that none of us wanted to be on.

'What are your aspirations for Superdry?' I asked Julian.

'I want my business to be like Ralph Lauren,' he replied, like a shot.

'Oh no, he has delusions of grandeur,' I thought. 'Superdry is not going to be the next Ralph Lauren. It doesn't have the bandwidth to reach those heights.'

Despite my early reservations, I still thought of Julian as a very entrepreneurial chap. He founded a company called Cult Clothing and had employed James to come up with new brands under the Cult Clothing umbrella. James spawned Superdry, which became very successful as a brand on its own, and inevitably Cult Clothing morphed into Superdry.

I was keen to finish the conversation as quickly as possible so I could get on with my job, and I felt that was reciprocated in the way we rapidly exchanged goodbyes.

Some months later, I read an article about Superdry taking over the Austin Reed flagship store on Regent Street. This was a big deal because Austin Reed was a monolithic British heritage brand whose patrons had included the Beatles, David Niven and Winston Churchill, to name a few. They were London's first department store for men and were just done celebrating their centennial year on Regent Street.

This was the first tangible link I could see between us and Superdry. Being at the end of Regent Street meant they were also within touching distance of Savile Row and Jermyn Street. Despite Superdry not having any kind of house tailoring, this new proximity connected the dots in my mind of what a collaboration could look like. I envisaged dysfunctional tailoring and dishevelled silhouettes called the 'Rock 'n' Rolla of Jermyn Street' and the 'Punk Rocker of Savile Row'.

I called James. Luckily, he remembered me from our forced introduction at Bread and Butter, a few months earlier. We agreed to meet up for a drink at Soho House, down Greek Street, the next day, where I pitched the idea to him of the 'Country Rebel'.

James turned up on-brand, wearing a Superdry biker's jacket, a grey Superdry logo tee and a pair of faded Superdry denims. He had some very nice blue suede Chelsea boots on, which I presumed he bought elsewhere. I ordered meatballs and a plant-based mac and cheese, and James had figs and a yellow coconut curry.

'I've got something to show you, James,' I said, once the burly waiter had taken our empty plates away. I took out two photos from my brown leather satchel and passed them to James. One photo was of an old Austin Reed poster showing a man in a 1920s-style brown suit with yellow and orange overchecks. The other was of a young Mick Jagger in the 1970 film *Performance*, where he starred as the reclusive eccentric rock star alongside James Fox. Jagger had his hair strewn past his cheeks and ears, with his fringe cut and parted in the centre. He wore a Carnaby Street tweed jacket to acknowledge his countryside surroundings and oozed an aloofness that exuded a very unique kind of cool.

James liked the idea in principle, but it required me to extrapolate, so I set about helping him visualise it. The designs needed to be interchangeable enough that you could wear with a hoodie, with a T shirt and with a pair of jeans.

Whenever I'm thinking about commercial projects, I always place myself in the shoes of the customer and work my way backwards. If the customer understands the concept, then everything else can be joined up.

A few days later, I invited James to our studio on Elder Street to show him some early mock-ups. I showed him a lovely green Harris tweed peppered with some purple heather-like hues which distinguished it from any normal-looking tweed. I'd sewn a yellow under-collar and navy cotton patches on the shoulder and elbow, but in unconventional shapes. It certainly took inspiration from the country, but it was far too foppish for hunting, shooting or fishing. I crudely but strategically cut Superdry patterns and Country Rebel badges on it, hung it on the mannequin and slapped Mick Jagger's face above it.

'Love it, Timothy, but how do we expand on this?' James asked.

I pulled out another photo; this time it was the Japanese poster of the 1960s movie *Our Man Flint*, an American spoof spy series that parodied James Bond. The Japanese graphics on the poster resonated with James as Superdry incorporate them unashamedly in their designs. The Super Spy silhouette was carved out of all my machinations of 1960s iconography from films of that era and TV series like *The Avengers* and *The Saint*.

The third look was a character we coined 'the Bank Robber', which largely riffed on Michael Caine's character in the 1970s British classic *Get Carter*. For most of the promo posters, Caine is seen holding a shotgun, sheathed in that impervious tonic suit by Doug Hayward, with bottle caps for cufflinks.

'Tim, this is really interesting,' James said eagerly, 'but we need to get Julian on board. If Julian buys into it, he'll back the whole thing.'

By the time Julian came down to Elder Street to inspect the concept, we had already mapped out the four characters and had blown up some posters creating something similar to a Superdry boutique. I didn't want to just show Julian a mood board of sketches and fabrics, I wanted him to see something tangible.

He sauntered around the easels and mannequins, muttering a few things inaudibly. Julian was quite withdrawn and didn't look overly enthused about any of it. He excused himself and went outside for a cigarette. He returned with a new vigour as if the nicotine had brought him a moment of clarity. He threw his coat on the chair and hung an arm around me.

'Tim, I'll be honest, I wasn't expecting anything at all. I thought this was going to be a waste of my time. But it's fantastic. I want to order 5,000 pieces as a trial.'

Superdry don't do tailoring, so it was up to me to find a supply chain. Fortunately, my friends in Turkey (who I knew through my factories in North London) were available and, as luck would have it, 60 per cent of what Superdry were producing was coming out of Turkey. It was quite serendipitous; they had an office in Istanbul and so it all tied together rather nicely.

Slapping Mick Jagger's face on a mannequin is one thing, but delivering on a project is where the real work begins. Julian and James had just taken on a new PR lady, Kat Jameson. She had just relocated back to Cheltenham and was ex-Gucci, so came with a good international pedigree.

I was impressed with her. She knew how to put a launch together and arranged the majority of the press, but the collection needed a proper event to get it off the ground. Coincidentally, Dylan Jones was just heading up London Collections: Men, a biannual showcase that takes place every January and June and celebrates the creative and commercial importance of the British menswear industry.

I knew it would elevate Superdry and distinguish it from its casualwear contemporaries. No one expected the likes of Superdry to be on the same stretch of carpet as Burberry or Craig Green.

When I paid Dylan a visit at his office at *Condé Nast*, he very receptive to my idea but had some reservations. 'I wouldn't mind doing it, Tim,' he said, 'but I'm not sure it fits in with our current line-up.'

'What do you mean?'

'Are you going to exhibit?'

'I hadn't planned on it.'

Dylan was wearing an off-white three-button collar shirt with mitred cuffs that he either failed to remember to button, or just felt they looked cool undone. That was one of the many things I liked about Dylan: he could be quirky with his clothes and, whether it was by accident or design, he still made it work.

'Well, we're not doing much in the East End. We'd love for you to do something out that way,' Dylan said.

It was a 'you scratch my back and I'll scratch yours' agreement. I would show in the East End and Dylan would get Superdry on the schedule.

Collectively, we had to think on how we could deliver this launch and make it such a spectacle that people would have to write about it. I had a great team at Timothy Everest, but equally, so did Julian and James. They blew up all the old Austin Reed posters I'd picked out back in the early mock-ups, altered some of the colours and embossed the name Timothy Everest over the suits.

On the floors we had blown up some paper patterns that I had originally made up as a collage in the fitting rooms back in Elder Street. Everything else was equally exaggerated and ambitious. Huge vintage cotton reels bookended the stage and large, banner-sized measuring tapes hung from the ceiling like bunting on coronation day. They were having fun with it, flexing their creative muscles and displaying all the experience they'd gleaned from doing festivals and exhibitions like Bread and Butter.

We went with my idea to present the collection like an art installation, forgoing the conventional catwalk show that was just a bit too stale for my liking. We procured an area on the first floor and dotted our characters around the visuals that the Superdry team had produced.

I put a mix tape together and instructed the models to change position at the end of each track so it wouldn't look stagnant. It was a trick I lifted from a Balenciaga exhibition I had seen years ago and had made quite an impression on me.

Catherine had started to make her own candles by this point, and we lit those to create an ambience. Outside of the venue we also wanted to drum up a little noise and enlisted Jamie Oliver to zoom around

Piccadilly in a Morgan three-wheeler that was heavily branded with the Superdry logo.

Jamie was a huge fan of Superdry; he invited me and the Superdry boys down to one of his restaurants in Cheltenham a few weeks before the exhibit. When I was introduced to him, he shook my hand and said in front of the whole team, 'You're not a wanker, are you, Tim?'

'I beg your pardon?' I said.

'I've being asking about you, Tim,' Jamie said. 'My wife used to be a model and tells me your business is full of wankers. Now, I've asked around, and people have put your name alongside the likes of Paul Smith and Christopher Bailey. So, you're alright, aren't you?'

'I suppose so,' I said, and we moved the conversation on to more interesting matters such as his restaurants and margins within his business.

Jamie later apologised to me for what he considered a rude introduction.

'Jamie, there is really no need,' I assured him. 'I actually thought you were quite charming and wanted to thank you for our frank conversation about your business.' We smiled, shook hands and openly agreed that the Morgan three-wheeler can entertain at a canter better than some cars manage at full pelt.

The event was a huge success. Everyone could buy into what we were doing, and the collection simply exploded. The press coined the campaign 'a real game changer' and Superdry's share price shot up on the back of it. The investors were already enamoured with Julian's ambition and his rhetoric of wanting to build a bigger business and their faith in him was repaid when they took the bull by the horns and moved from Cheltenham to one of the most prestigious locations in London, the aforementioned flagship store on Regent Street. As time goes by, I do think they might have forgotten how much difference to the company we made, being part of the Superdry aura at that time and propelling the good publicity that surrounded the company.

To generate good PR and good publicity it's imperative that one must celebrate the good news when it comes around. I soon cottoned on to this back in 1999 when M&S got riddled with bad press after axing British suppliers Daks-Simpson and William Baird in a bid to make cheaper clothes abroad. They were getting a real hammering, but their company line was to keep rolling out the same tired mantra, 'We produce abroad to remain competitive on the high street'. Instead of defending their decision, they should have been highlighting and celebrating the fact that M&S were still making more clothes in the UK than any other high-street store. Always talk louder about the good news than you do the bad.

I was still consulting with M&S at this time as Superdry was not one of the brands in my non-compete. On the back of our success story with Superdry, I was hoping to impress the powers that be at M&S with what is possible when you think slightly out of the box. But that never happened, and I eventually cut ties and decided to put all my efforts into Superdry.

Meanwhile, Goatee had begun courting me for a working relationship. He had just been let go by Julian and James, and I was entertaining the idea of bringing him on board to deal with all my administration. The idea appealed to me because it would allow me to get on with what I was good at.

I was on a trip with Goatee, talking things through about what a working relationship would look like when I got a phone call from James. 'Tim, I'll get right to it,' James stamped. 'I want to thank you for everything. It has been absolutely brilliant working alongside you. But Julian and I, well we've been thinking about it, we don't want to continue our working relationship with you.'

'Oh,' I said. This caught me off-guard. I wanted to ask James what their reasoning was. I was sure that, whatever their issue was for breaking it off, could be resolved, or at least discussed and worked around.

'We're going in a different direction,' James added.

'A different direction?' I thought. 'Why do we need to go off-piste from the success that we've generated by working together?' 'That's a shame. We've done a good job haven't we?'

'Goodbye, Tim.' Click.

Fuck it. This was going to hit us hard. I knew it at the time. Losing the income from M&S meant we were taking on water. The Superdry link had stopped the bleeding but losing that too in quick succession put us into a spiral. Although it was perfectly amicable (perhaps too amicable), I hadn't really figured out the true reason behind James and Julian calling time on our little venture. The abrupt, sickly politeness of it all left me confused and gobsmacked.

It wasn't until two years later, when I accidentally bumped into Julian in New York, that I got to the bottom of it all. I was in town for a trade fair and combined the trip, like I normally do, with seeing private clients for fittings. On my afternoon off, I ventured down to one of my favourite haunts, the Meat Packing District. There I was poolside, having dinner with some friends on the top floor of Soho House (the very same Soho House that Samantha failed to talk her way into in an episode of *Sex and the City*), when – sod's law – in walk Julian and James accompanied by maybe eight or so very glamorous girls.

'This is too good an opportunity to miss,' I thought. But it would look a little ungainly gate-crashing their party. I needed it to look very casual, like we were just bumping into each other back on Regent Street. Nonchalantly, I took an unnecessary detour to the bar, then round the back to the loos, which led me back to the other side.

'Wow,' said James as our eyes locked.

'James, what a surprise!' I said, embracing him and slightly relieved that he was pleased to see me. He introduced me warmly to all the girls. Julian said hello but grimaced a little. Something was off with Julian and had been for a number of years.

After a few drinks and a bit of Dutch courage, we excused ourselves from the group to have a man-to-man, out of earshot on the far side of the pool.

'How's it going, mate?' he asked.

'Good thanks, are you having a good time?'

'Why did you fucking do that?' he shot, opening his palms.

'Why did I fucking do what?'

'Why did you get into bed with Goatee? You know, when I found out, it was like you were stabbing me in the heart.' Julian put down his drink and pointed his finger. His finger must have been within an inch of my chin. 'You know he tried to take me out of my business. He tried to do a boardroom coup and take me out of my own business. Me! I founded the bloody thing. He won't know what the fuck to do with your business, Tim. I taught him everything. He is a tricky fucker and you should watch him.'

Julian holstered his finger and didn't say anything more about it. We had a nice chat afterwards about the benefits of being a member of Soho

House. I'd always liked Julian, I liked his 'think big, be big' mentality. In hindsight, I can appreciate what he was trying to convey regarding wanting to be like Ralph Lauren. He wanted Superdry to be a global brand that could have a product portfolio big enough to house many different brands. His aspiration was to get to a billion dollars. It's a shame we never got to carry on working after that, but you never know what's round the corner, as I was about to find out.

22

Teaming Up with Goatee

A sinkhole appeared in Courtenay Road, Poole, on Tuesday, March 14 after a car drove over it as it was reversing out of a driveway.

Bournemouth Echo

The brand Timothy Everest was about to have its 25th anniversary. We were established, with a good reputation, we hadn't burnt any bridges and I felt there was enough terra firma to bring in a partner who could propel the business forward in ways that I couldn't.

These kind of elevations in business will typically come down to two resources, human and financial. The tricky part in our industry is that when one thinks creatively in the business, it's often in an artistic sense and seldom from a financial aspect. The finance people focus purely on bottom lines, while the designers are consumed with what shape their next collection will take.

The finance people will always focus more on when they are going to see a return on their investment. And when it comes to investors, you've got to be careful that you don't end up working for them, even though you have a similar or better shareholding. These thoughts were bubbling away like trapped air gurgling in a car radiator stuck in traffic.

One morning, I got a call from Goatee while in my study. 'Timothy, do you have a minute?' he asked. Between my name and the question there was a pregnant pause, which informed me he had something that would take longer than a minute. I coiled up my empty bag of mini cheddars and slid it neatly between the press of my desktop hole puncher.

'I'm listening, but I do have one foot out of the door,' I lied, slowly closing the clamp on the hole puncher with my palm.

'I'd like to get involved in a business, something like yours. I can bring all of my knowledge I've gained over the years from launching my own business shop and working with Superdry over to Timothy Everest.'

At this point, I was under the illusion that Goatee had left Superdry on his own volition. The reality was that Julian and James had kicked him out, but I wasn't to know that then.

'We can have a more elevated proposition,' Goatee went on, 'and I can help you scale the business.'

Goatee gave me his pitch over the next few minutes. To his credit, it was a good one, but I wasn't overly enamoured with the idea of Goatee running the show. I pulled the wrapper free from the hole puncher, lifted it to my eyes like one would with a tiny set of binoculars designed for the opera and peered through the tiny holes.

'Let's go to Amsterdam and we'll talk it over. We'll get the wives together, it's my 50th birthday so we'll fly private. You game?'

'I'll have to think about it,' I said, and rang off.

Flying private to Amsterdam doesn't sound like much of a spoil, considering it's only an hour and twenty minutes from Heathrow, but it's still a wonderful experience despite not being the most eco-friendly way to travel.

We all got on very well. I was starting to like Goatee and I was beginning to see how much of a charmer he was. Having worked for Tommy and Malcolm, I knew only too well that having some charm up your sleeve can be a valuable asset in business. He brought along his wife, and she and Catherine hit it off immediately, helped by a few bottles of bubbly of course.

We did talk a little business on the plane, and Goatee's wife cut across us and contributed, 'It's great you guys are getting on, but you know money really fucks things up in the end.'

When we touched down in Amsterdam, I got that call from James at Superdry. The 'different direction' call. The 'letting you go' call. The 'you're now fucked' call.

Talk about a crash landing. That call certainly sobered me up, although I kept the news to myself for the duration of the trip.

Losing both M&S and Superdry in rapid-fire succession had radically reduced my choices for moving the business forward. We either had to make people redundant to reduce overheads, which would have stymied the company's growth considerably, or find some new investment very quickly. We were the clothing equivalent of a film production company that had lost the movie but still had all the actors and extras on set waiting for me to call 'action!'

This knee to the nuts from Superdry inevitably accelerated us towards Goatee's proposition. When we returned to London, I took Catherine out for dinner and explained not only losing the Superdry deal, but Goatee's proposition.

'Do we jump?' I asked. 'Or do we just stick where we are, downsize and live to fight another day?'

Catherine demurred. 'We're short on options,' she said. 'Yes, we could downsize and that might help the balance sheet in the short term, but from the outside looking in, it never breeds confidence when the company's trajectory is seen to be on a downward curve. You've always been proud of having a good reputation, delivering on campaigns and bolstering other people's businesses in the process. But what's more, you're very sentimental when it comes to the people who have been loyal to you.'

When we returned to the house, I paced around my study and found myself inexplicably flipping a pound coin like one of those sociopaths you see in comic-book movies. I called Goatee. 'Let's do it,' I said. I was taking a calculated punt on keeping a good public persona, although this was very much going against my gut instinct.

'Let's really do it, Tim,' Goatee agreed, and I hung up. I fumbled the coin and it landed with a dull clink on the parquet flooring before rolling irretrievably under the dressing table.

The £1 deal

Having agreed quite good terms initially, Goatee drove some very strong bargains at the end. In the world of business, they call it 'ending' when you agree one thing and then they change it when they've got you to the finish line. Presumably because it feels like much harder work to pedal back on the deal and start over than it does to begrudgingly accept a weaker position to move things along. Ironic, really – they call it 'ending' when you're just entering a new partnership.

Various other names were introduced into the fold. The ones I liked were substituted at the last minute for others whom I didn't like from day one. Still, semi-reluctantly but knowing full well the implications, I sat down with Goatee and signed the deal.

'I'm putting a lot of trust in you, Goatee,' I said, scribbling my life away.

Goatee's bottom lip popped outwards as he nodded in acknowledgement. He started to roll up his sleeves as a symbolic gesture, but then thought better of it and rolled them back.

A few months later, we launched our first collection under the new partnership. It became quite apparent to me from the get-go that Goatee, from a product perspective, knew next to nothing about brands. He seemed to assume that just putting a collection together under the banner Timothy Everest would ensure its instant success. In reality, launching a successful collection is the result of an amalgamation of doing a lot of tedious stuff exceptionally well.

'I might not understand brands, Timothy,' Goatee admitted (but only after I pulled him up on it), 'but I do understand business.'

That curt rebuttal sent a mini shockwave to my core. It transported me momentarily to an incident I witnessed some years back when I was having a drink with Lloyd in a pub down the West End.

In one end of the pub, I caught the eye of Stuart 'The Saint' Trevor, co-founder of the brand AllSaints. Stuart was there with his team but not in a very convivial sense. There was a scowl on his face and it was directed to a huddle of men in sharp pinstripe suits, laughing and rollicking at the other end of the bar. Among the pinstripes was the fashion financier Kevin Stanford, co-founder of Karen Millen. Not long after, I read in the papers that Kevin bought out all the partners of AllSaints, besides Stuart, becoming the major shareholder. He then bought out Stuart and ultimately, as so often is the case with these buyouts, everybody lost everything.

Goatee was not the driving force I expected him to be in the business. Although, if there was one thing he was crash-hot on, it was my expense account and my apparent abuse of the company's petty cash.

'Timothy. I can't make out this ATM receipt at Heston Services. What's going on? What were you doing there of all places?' he said over the phone to me one morning.

'Goatee, I got a taxi to the airport last week when I flew to Japan. I had to get the money out from somewhere.'

'You got a taxi to the airport?' he gasped, in the same way an auditor would gasp at an expense bill for £5,000 spent at the casino in Les Ambassadeurs.

'Yes, a taxi. You can't expect me to hitchhike down the M4 from Richmond to Terminal 5. For one, it's illegal; for two, it's ridiculous.'

'There's no need to get chippy, Timmy. We just need to put the brakes on. We can't keep burning through all—'

'Goatee,' I said, shutting him down. 'I don't do chippy, and I don't take kindly to having my day disrupted. You chasing me for twenty sheets is really putting the *petty* into petty cash. Surely the investment here is to actually find some business. What are you doing to help us find new business? Figure that one out and call me back.' I slung the phone down, and, without a second's thought, poured myself a long Glenfiddich and drank it down. It was 10.20 a.m. and I was feeling quite rotten.

My anxieties were starting to mount, but not as much as the sums that were being spent on the business from the finance side.

'How much is the tally up to, Tim?' Lloyd asked curiously, his eyes gun barrel straight into mine.

'I can't tell you, because I don't know exactly. But it's a lot, and it doesn't feel right,' I said sheepishly.

Lloyd picked up his shears and began to cut away at a long bolt of Black Watch tartan. 'It's not a good scenario, Tim. I think there's a premeditated, calculated play here. He's moving his pieces around the board, charming the opposing pawns to his side, and sooner or later you'll be in check mate.'

Over the course of the coming months, Goatee started to pile on the pressure financially. My shoulders were quite literally sagging as I moped around the shop like a second-hand punchbag. Each morning, I threw on my suit jacket before leaving the house, and each morning, it felt heavier than the day before.

I wasn't being entirely truthful with Lloyd. I knew exactly what the tally was up to. Goatee had used his company to lend money to the business vehicle that we owned together. And this vehicle, with its back on fire, was running up a debt of at least seven figures.

To inject some cash into the business, I struck up a partnership with Rolls-Royce. I was scheduled to do a presentation down in their showroom on Berkeley Square one Friday night, and with one foot out of the door, I got handed a legal letter that stipulated an answer was required by Monday morning.

It's the oldest trick in the playbook of bully-boy corporates. Spoil their weekend, make them feel uncomfortable. Goatee's company, which had invested in Timothy Everest, wanted its money back. Effectively, he was defaulting on himself, and if we couldn't pay back the money of his company's investment, he'd enforce an administration.

Sure enough, the following Monday morning, I went to see Goatee at his flat. He was sat behind his desk, which was cluttered with heaps and heaps of red-top newspapers and empty triangle sandwich cartons. Sat either side of Goatee were two men in suits made of cheap boiled black wool.

'Are you going to accept leaving the company?' Goatee asked. 'Because otherwise I'm going to put it into administration.'

'Goatee, I would have appreciated some forewarning about the agenda of this meeting 'cos had I known you'd bring your henchmen along, I would have brought my PPK.'

'Timothy, you knew this was coming. The company is going down the plughole,' Goatee said.

'Why do you want to get rid of your best asset?' I said. 'I'm your best asset. My name is above the door.'

'Well, actually that might be the case,' said one of the black suits, removing his glasses and resting them on the bulldog clip of his clipboard, 'but my client believes the name above the door is much more important than you. He doesn't need you in the business. He's got the experience to take the business to the next level, I'm sorry Mr Everest.'

'That's Sir Timothy Everest to you,' I said, for the first time in my life. 'And next time you turn up for a meeting as big as this, might I recommend you come see me for a suit first. That goes for you an' all.'

I swung my finger between the two henchmen. 'This is not a big established business like your Paul Smiths or Ralph Laurens of the world. This is a small family business and you're taking it out with a bloody nuclear bomb.'

'Timothy, the alternatives don't bear thinking about,' Goatee said, and then there was silence. The cold reality hung in the air like a bad cliff-hanger to an awful episode of some dreary daytime drama.

Some months later, I reluctantly agreed to leave the business and signed the papers served to me by another one of Goatee's henchmen from compliance. Goatee was too cowardly to be there in person to see me sign. At least this henchman had a better suit on him, I thought.

'I'm sorry, Mr Everest. I don't like doing this,' the well-dressed hench-man said, and I believed him. 'It's just my job, you understand?'

'Well, you shouldn't be doing a job you don't like. And what you're doing here, young man, is really quite nasty.'

I signed my name and business away for £1. After twenty-five years of graft, that's all they gave us. One. Measly. Pound. It was the most galling thing I've ever done in my life.

The henchman patched me through to Goatee, who was on his yacht somewhere off the Greek coast. 'Thank you, Timothy,' he said, the sea wind distorting the loudspeaker. 'I'll look after this business, and we'll do a good job. Your legacy is in safe hands.'

The henchman slid a pound coin across the table and couldn't bring himself to look me in the eye.

'Remember, Goatee, just because you've made money in one job, doesn't mean you have the Midas touch,' I said and rang off. I picked up the pound coin and flicked it back at the young henchman, who caught it sublimely. 'Give that to your favourite charity,' I said.

'No, Mr Everest. We have to give you this pound!'

I walked out of the room. Behind me the henchman called out over my shoulder, 'We've got to be seen paying for this business!'

The words rang up and down the walls of the corridor. By the time I got home, Goatee had wired £1 to my bank account.

The fallout of all this was, quite frankly, an absolute fucking mess. There was the obvious stuff like being shut out from my own email and social media accounts and various whispers and lies in what the company told my personal clients about my mysterious departure. But the Goatee-shaped forest fire that ripped through the business would never have caught light had I not lit the match. I signed the deals. I pulled the plug that drained the swamp, and you can't begrudge whatever monster crawls out to fight tooth and nail for its own survival.

The contract I signed prevented me from doing anything with the name Timothy Everest and doing any kind of tailoring or talking openly about the business for a whole year. Inevitably, I'd have customers call and they'd ask what was going on. I became well versed in fudging the issue and deflecting it quickly onto another topic of conversation.

* * *

The main headache of starting all over again was not being able to leverage the cachet that came with my own name. We couldn't sing about all the great things we'd done in the past.

After a while, I was getting a bit restless and came round to a different way of thinking. No matter what the non-compete form I signed said, one cannot simply wipe away history and common knowledge. The things we accomplished as a brand are out there in the public domain, and to deny my own involvement in the success story of Timothy Everest would not only be dishonest, but very silly.

This moment of sobriety sparked enough confidence in me to pick up a little bit of trade to help tread some water. However, without my team I could only take on a maximum of two projects, Lucan Menswear and La Martina, a polo shirt brand. I'm sure this rang fire bells back at Timothy Everest, where Goatee was now pulling the strings, because of the backlash that was about to happen.

One night in Berlin, I was due to host a dinner for La Martina on behalf of German *GQ*. With one foot out of my hotel door, I went to pull up the address for the venue on my phone only to find that all my emails had completely vanished. All of my contacts were gone.

'Fuck!' I said, loud enough to bring a shake of the head from an elderly couple camped out in the lobby.

'*Entschuldigung Sie bitte,*' I said.

I had no idea where this place was and I had to be at the venue in an hour. Biting the bullet, I calmly rang the La Martina head office, and a friendly female voice answered the phone.

'Timothy Everest here in Berlin. I'm just on my way to the venue, only the address has fallen off the email thread, do you happen to have it there?' Fortunately, the young girl pulled through and I got to the venue just in time, albeit destabilised and a little flustered.

Just as I envisaged, the Japanese did not take kindly to news of me no longer being at Timothy Everest. And believe me, I know if the panic bells were ringing in Japan they could be heard twice as loudly back in London. Goatee asked for a meeting at Soho House, and I agreed.

'No henchman today, Goatee?' I asked sardonically, shaking his hand.

'Think what you want of me, Timothy. I'm trying to salvage this business. The Japanese are losing it. I need you to go over there and smooth things over.'

'Before we get into any of that, I need a drink,' I said, and Goatee summoned a waiter over with a click of his four chubby fingers. The waiter, with an unsightly amount of dandruff in his short beard, shuttled over so promptly that I assumed he had either no self-esteem or was just very eager to please.

'Bring me your most expensive bottle of red wine from the Rhône Valley,' I said, 'and one glass.'

'Would sir like to see the wine list? Or rather speak to our sommelier?' asked Dandruff.

'No, thank you. To make it simple, just bring me the bottle of Côte Rôtie Domaine and a bag of scampi fries,' I said. Goatee dismissed the waiter with a knowing look.

'Look, Tim,' Goatee said, hunching forward. 'I'll give you £5,000 to go to Japan for one week. Think of it as a paid holiday. Hang out with old client friends, kiss each other's arses, and tell them all is good this side of the water.'

'You're offering me £5,000 to go over to Japan to save a business worth six figures?' I asked.

We locked horns for a spell before Dandruff interjected and placed the wine bottle and bag of scampi fries on the table between us. I took the bag of scampi fries and squirrelled them into the pocket of my chore jacket. 'You'll have to do better than that five grand, Goatee,' I said, and left.

After some increased offers, and a few days of back and forths with the directors, I relented. I called Goatee.

'I'll go,' I said.

'Thank you, Tim,' he said, more relieved than grateful.

'But I won't be doing it forever. It's tough trying to flog your own name, you know, especially as someone else will be the beneficiary.'

'I know,' he said. He thanked me again, and I hung up.

23

Start All Over

It's recommended, when getting back behind the wheel after a long time out, to plan an easy journey and not to let other drivers pressure you.

When I returned from Japan, I had a meeting with fellow creative Danny Kellard. Danny was a down to earth, affable chap who loved his Negronis and had every single shade of grey and ginger in his beard. He had one foot in the advertising communications industry and the other in anything and everything creative. We moved quickly on a partnership scheme with the working title Mr. Tim, which would later morph into MBE Studios.

If we were going to start afresh then we needed a change of scenery, so we upped sticks from Elder Street and launched the new business at Number One Fashion Street.

Once we moved in, I decided to step on the PR accelerator, but because of my gag order, I had to do a lot of deflection around the real reason for stepping down from Timothy Everest. This included rebuking all rumours circling about me moving out because I did not want to invest in the maintenance of the building.

One journalist I spoke to, however, already had the inside track on what really happened. 'You got Nuttered, Tim,' he said bombastically, in reference to what finally happened to Tommy when he lost control of his business, although Tommy's situation was vastly different. Tommy gave most of his shares in his business to his investors, who consequently voted him out. In my view, what happened to me was far more pernicious.

'Can I put that bit in, Tim?' the journalist asked. 'It would be great if I could say you got "Nuttered" in the last paragraph of the piece.'

I told him no but I did appreciate that he had the courtesy to ask. 'We've got to be bigger than that,' I said. 'No one wants to hear bad news, and they can read the red tops if it's gossip they're after. Just say it was a tsunami of shit, born of my own doing, and my shoulders must be the shoreline to take the brunt.'

Had Goatee gone on to make Timothy Everest a huge successful empire, then I would have held my hands up and confessed that all the decisions made to evict me from the business were the right ones. But that hasn't happened. My biggest fear now is that Timothy Everest will disintegrate entirely and just dwindle off, survived only by small concessions in department stores such as House of Fraser.

We launched a website to help promote MBE Studios and it helped paint the story of what we had achieved in the past as Timothy Everest. A week later, after another jaunt in Japan promoting Timothy Everest, the brand, I received another red letter from Goatee's lawyers informing me that I was infringing on *his* intellectual property. The red letter instructed me in no uncertain terms that I should not be talking about my filmography, my past clientele, my numerous visits to Pinewood or anything else that might pass off as me being Timothy Everest. It was just plain bonkers. When Tom Ford, the man, sells Tom Ford, the business, how is he going to refer to his time working on the James Bond films?

I ripped up the letter and did the same with all the others that followed – which is something that I should have done from the very beginning. Goatee would dispatch me to Japan to help drive sales, then look to incarcerate me the minute I landed back on British soil.

Eventually, I drew a line in the sand. I did my last trunk show in Japan supporting Timothy Everest, which was emotionally charged. I felt like a jilted lover having gone through a messy divorce only to go back for the kind of trysts that leave a bad taste in the back of one's mouth.

They say one door closes and another door opens. With Timothy Everest, I was trapped in a revolving door waiting to be spat out on the cold concrete. But another door was about to open, and I got a call one morning that I took in the hallway of my home.

'Hello, is that Timothy Everest?' a man asked in a very concise manner.

'Yes, who is this?'

'My name is Richard. I want to talk to you about buying my business Grey Flannel.'

Grey Flannel

Richard Froomberg came from a family of retailers and clothing manufacturers. He was a desk boy working in London but found himself out of a job when the economy collapsed in 1973. Still, he was able to use his business brain to revive the fortunes of Grey Flannel, an ailing casual menswear business on Chiltern Street that was only twelve months old.

Very rapidly, Richard built a substantial reputation that redesigned the look for menswear in the UK during the mid-seventies. Richard would have his design team create their own fabrics and have his collections manufactured in Switzerland to his own, very unique specifications.

They would have Americans visit the Grey Flannel shop during the buying season, clean out the shelves and mimic Richard's designs for their own markets back in the US. This would upset many brands and designers, and understandably so, but Richard took it all in his stride. 'Imitation is the best form of flattery,' he would tell me, years later. 'And the best compliment someone can pay you is when they pay you. By the time brands rolled out their version of what I was doing, their buyers would have already bank-rolled the one I would be working on next.'

Richard was always very clever when it came to selling merchandise. Before every buying season, he would ensure all the different product groups followed a strict colour scheme so that if someone came in for a shirt, they could buy a pair of trousers or jacket to match.

My love affair with and reverence for Grey Flannel began when I worked for Malcolm, mainly because they were on the same street as us, just one door down. They were the early pioneers of buying in brands like Giorgio Armani, and they put together the kind of collections where the customer came first – a simple ploy, the importance of which has been completely lost or forgotten with some retailers in the past few years. Far too often, I see merchandisers throw in uncoordinated collections and brands in the hope of creating trends they want to set. For casualwear, that approach is a fool's errand, believe me.

When one finds themselves on Chiltern Street, one will be hard pressed not to be seduced by its quaint village-like beauty. At one end of the street there is Chiltern Firehouse, a redbrick Edwardian castle, which was the oldest fire station in London until it was decommissioned in 2005. Now it serves as a hotel and restaurant, famed for its daily rollcall of A-list diners. Opposite is Shreeji News, for my money, one of the best specialist magazine and news publication shops in all of London. A stone's throw from the Firehouse is the Wallace Collection, home to Frans Hals' *The Laughing Cavalier*. Although Jean-Honoré Fragonard's *The Swing* is my personal favourite. It depicts an elegant lady on a swing being pushed by her layman husband, who is being cuckolded by a man hiding in the bushes.

Chiltern Street is littered with boutique stores and cafés and when I ventured over to meet with Richard to discuss business it dawned on me that there is a whole world over there that is rarely frequented by the gentlemen of Shoreditch.

Around 2010, when Malcolm's shop became available, I had considered setting up shop in Chiltern Street. However, Sunspel swooped in and have since made a wonderful space there.

After my meeting with Richard, I fell in love with Grey Flannel all over again. I wanted in.

The shop needed a bit of TLC, but the brand still had great pedigree, it was in an enviable location, and I could run my operations for MBE Studios downstairs as a subsidiary and bespoke arm of Grey Flannel. There was a small problem, however. I was already tied into a lease over in Fashion Street with my friend Chris and didn't want to renege on our commitments to him. We were intrinsic to Chris, moving out would deeply affect his bottom line and I didn't fancy pissing him off as we were good mates.

Then, out of nowhere – Covid-19. Every shop and small business in the UK was forced to close, batten down the hatches and wait for further instructions.

I called Lloyd. 'Lloyd, we're fucked. What do we do now?'

'Call Chris,' he said. 'Get a read on what's going on with the building.'

I called Chris. 'Chris, can you believe what's going on?'

'I know,' he said. 'The world is on fire and upside down, Tim. They've even called off the Premier League matches!'

'Where does that leave us?'

'Well, I think they'll start playing them behind closed doors, so it shouldn't be too bad.'

'I meant, where does that leave us with regard to the shop?'

'Oh,' Chris audibly inhaled. 'Well, Tim, it's not great news I'm afraid. I've got a bit of an embarrassing situation. We're going to need some of the space back. You see, the businesses above and below you need to implement this social-distancing bullcrap. Basically, the same people need double the space. Is there any chance we can move you to a smaller office, and be appointment only?'

Those words sounded like they came from one of those wind-up vintage music boxes. Arresting and angelic.

'Chris, would it be easier for you if I wasn't there at all?'

'Well, yes,' he said. 'But what are you going to do? I don't want to chuck you out on the street, Tim.'

'Don't worry about me, I'll work it out.' I rang off and called Richard. We worked out a very favourable deal that didn't cost us a lot but gave us a chance to begin again properly. Richard probably didn't get as much as he'd have liked, but he did get to leave a legacy of a business which is now over fifty years old, something he has great reason to be proud of. The deal we struck also had a clause that meant if we did a good job with Grey Flannel, Richard would be fairly compensated. So, once again, we were about to embark on a new adventure. And still the adventure goes on.

Join the Club

After we negotiated that tricky spell of Covid-19 that most shopkeepers call 'the black years', Grey Flannel resurfaced with renewed optimism for the future. It gave me an opportunity to reflect on what I really wanted to do and where I wanted to be.

I managed to crystallise how I saw the brand and I conveyed to my team to think of us now as veteran tennis players, close to retirement but still capable of winning tournaments.

'How do you mean?' Lloyd said, peering over his frames.

'Well, we can still hit a kick serve,' I said. 'We can lob and drop shot from the back of the court, and we can remember that match winner.' I gesticulated, mimicking swings with tiny waves of my palm as if I was Rod Laver playing Arthur Ashe. 'But we can't outrun these younger guns or get mixed up in forty-shot rallies. We have to be really careful that we don't come across as *trying* to be youthful and trendy. At the same time, we mustn't talk about being old or how things were so much better during the mid-nineties.'

'But everything *was* better in the nineties,' Lloyd said.

'I know, Lloyd, but we gotta keep our traps shut about certain things.'

My intuition with Grey Flannel led us on a journey where we could dovetail Grey Flannel with what we were doing downstairs with MBE Studios. We could still offer the customer an off-the-peg wardrobe, while tailoring a complete wardrobe with made to measure.

As people were looking to travel more, we started to create an aspirational side of the brand, Club Flannel. We kickstarted with a soft launch, just a baseball cap that said 'Club Flannel' on it. Then we released a t-shirt and a travel bag and eventually started filling the shop windows with items that would get people excited once more about going on holiday. We wanted them to envisage how good they would look standing around a pool having a passion fruit martini, wearing Club Flannel clothing.

The name Club Flannel was derived from a simple conceit. We thought of Club, as in one of those swanky private members' clubs you'll find in Mayfair or Kensington. You don't want to be trying to get in when your name's not down on the door. We wanted people to feel included.

Danny came up with a very neat strapline, 'Club Flannel, Join In'. It would be largely fronted by Max, our young store manager who is also Danny's son, and Alyssia, my daughter, who was becoming a tailor in her own right. It would look fresh-faced enough to be contemporary, but with myself, Lloyd and a veteran sales team (Graham and another Danny) in the background to offer enough grey hair and gravitas to bolster the business.

'We have to look upwards,' I carried on telling my team. 'We're constantly down on what others are doing, our heads in our phones copying what's come before. We need to lead by example, quit judging and just get on with being the benchmark for quality. If we do all that, people will want to join us. And they'll help us. Everything we're doing at the moment is a reaction to conversations we've already had with our clients when we discuss the future. It's just like Marco Pierre White and his extortionate one lobster ravioli. We're just going to make sure that we do everything better than anyone else.' The team nodded, and we discussed more light-hearted things, like upcoming photoshoots in the Italian Riviera.

A few weeks later, we all flew out to Lake Maggiore to do a photoshoot for Club Flannel. There, I got talking to a friend about classic cars and whether the likes of RM Sotheby's would find themselves in shtook in ten years' time because tyre-kickers like me might not be around to appreciate them as much. We came to the conclusion that tailoring and the motor industry cross-pollinate more than one might think. Whether one is replacing the spark plugs on an old Jaguar, rebuilding the engine crank on one's 1980s Honda motorbike or inserting a jacket lining into a bespoke suit, it's all about provenance. It's about understanding the journey and getting the next generation engaged so that they can take on the life skills needed to keep the industry thriving.

I'm still an old romantic at heart. I like to talk about cars, where I've come from and what I've seen along the way. If the fan belt goes, that's life, and I'm sure I can perform a temporary fix on the side of a road somewhere. I want to feel the gears, hear the guttural splutter of the exhaust as I tap the accelerator and taste the oysters down in whatever restaurant I find myself when I reach my destination. What will I be wearing when I get there?

Le Mans racing driver Gregor Fisken told me a story once about when he stopped off to have some shirts made on the way to Targa Florio, an endurance automobile race in the mountains of Sicily. I remember thinking at the time, 'That's just so fucking cool'. And I still do.

The End

Author's Notes
– Peter Brooker

I managed to snare an interview with Timothy Everest for my previous book that I co-authored, *From Tailors With Love: An Evolution of Menswear Through the Bond Films.* From there, we stayed in touch and Timothy was always kind enough to come on to my podcast to give me the broad strokes on his involvement with making suits and costumes for *Mission Impossible, The Man From U.N.C.L.E.*, etc.

When I pitched the idea to Timothy that we should write a book about his life in tailoring, I was genuinely surprised when he said yes. Partly because I knew he had just launched a new business with Grey Flannel and MBE Studios and also because who wants to give their life story when their next big adventure is just ahead of them?

The interviews were initially carried out in person. I would drive from Chiswick, park up at Marylebone and walk over to see Timothy at the Grey Flannel shop. I'm a huge advocate for interviewing people in person, but the visits were short-lived once I had received a fixed-penalty notice for blocking a box junction somewhere just off Baker Street. All subsequent interviews were conducted over video call. Of course, with the Internet being quite flaky, here in London, it meant that every call had a truncated transcription of, 'Oh sorry, just lost you, Tim,' or 'You cut out there, what were you saying about Tom Cruise?'

It was very evident, hearing Timothy talk about his life, how his passion for tailoring was only equalled by his obsession with bicycles and motor vehicles. Concurrently, I was reading *Funeral in Berlin* by Len Deighton. Deighton always prefaced each chapter with a line or two about chess. These tiny inserts would cryptically foreshadow the outcome of the narrative so I adopted this technique for this book and incorporated some motor-racing-based metaphors wherever I could.

We didn't really have a plan when it came to telling the story. I just plonked the Dictaphone on the table between us and Timothy started with 'Well, I'd better just start from the beginning.' Timothy spoke so articulately, and his stories were so rich, that I was initially concerned that my job would be merely that of a latter-day receptionist, frantically transcribing the stories as they came. To a certain degree, that was the extent of my role for this book. I might reward myself with the title of ghost writer, but my job only involved capturing the jigsaw pieces as they fell from Timothy's memory, turning them all face up, finding the edges, and then we filled it in together. In truth, the jigsaw fell almost ready-made from the box, thanks to Timothy being such a great storyteller.

Timothy did give me carte blanche to interpret some dialogue to push the story forward. As you might have guessed, some artistic licence has been taken with the prose, but who can seriously remember every word that was said in a conversation yesterday, let alone forty years ago? While a line or two may have been added for the benefit of drama (admittedly with a Michael Caine inflection), the facts, the meetings, the situations and the outcomes have not been massaged.

A quick story, if you'll indulge me as I leave you. The very first session I had with Timothy when we began the journey, we chatted at his MBE Studios, underneath Grey Flannel on Chiltern Street. I tentatively pressed record, and off Timothy went. I can't remember me asking him a single question. It was fascinating and entertaining, and I was just praying that the recorder was working as Timothy showed no signs of pausing for thought.

After about twenty minutes in, I felt like I needed a bathroom break after a hot Monocle coffee had gone straight through me. 'No worries,' I thought, I'll just wait for a break in play and excuse myself. Thirty minutes passed, then forty minutes. There didn't seem to be a window where I could cut across Timothy and ask to be excused.

I was now at breaking point and Timothy was still on a roll! Forty-five minutes, fifty minutes. Christ, Tim! Stop talking. I have to go. My bladder's river of piss is about to burst its banks.

After an hour was up, I had no choice. I cut across Tim mid-sentence and told him I needed a toilet break. 'I'm a 43-year-old man, I'm not going to piss myself,' I said to myself, trying to look cool and walking with a leisurely stroll down the short hallway to the bathroom. No need to panic. However, my confidence in my own bladder control was sorely misplaced. What was worse, I was wearing a pair of stone-coloured cotton trousers that I had just bought from Timothy, and there was now a huge piss patch that was sponging its way down from my crotch towards my inner thigh.

The next ten minutes I spent in that bathroom, trying to towel-dry my nether regions, were the longest I'd ever spent in a tailor's toilet. I sheepishly came out and returned to the interview, shirt untucked, my panama straw hat 'strategically placed'.

Timothy was either too much of a gentleman to bring it up or perhaps too wrapped up in the telling of his upbringing to notice my mishap. I strongly believe the former. Still, we carried on like nothing had happened. Suffice to say, for all further sessions I came dressed in darker trousers and ensured that I frequented the bathroom before we hit record.

I'd like to thank Timothy and his team at Grey Flannel for enduring me and trusting me in helping him put his story down on paper. I'd like to thank my publisher, Mark Beynon, for taking a punt on both Timothy and me; my girlfriend Anastasia for listening to me whine, yet again, about life while living the dream in the centre of the universe; and finally, my dear old mum for keeping up the tradition of proofreading all my early drafts and highlighting the howlers before they saw the light of day.

Resources

Chapter 1

buildingourpast.com/2017/01/15/the-legacy-of-j-hepworth-son/comment-page-1/ (accessed 16 October 2022).

www.leeds-live.co.uk/best-in-leeds/whats-on-news/lost-leeds-nightclubs-pubs-miss-19357785 (accessed 16 May 2023).

nightclubhalloffame.com/portfolio-item/peter-stringfellow/ (accessed 16 May 2023).

drivingfast.net/racing-line/ (accessed 15 May 2023).

Chapter 2

www.yorkshirepost.co.uk/heritage-and-retro/heritage/salts-mill-symbol-industrial-heritage-jonathan-silver-transformed-thriving-hub-arts-and-commerce-1744001 (accessed 16 October 2022).

digital.nls.uk/1980s/society/london-culture/ (accessed 17 October 2022).

42ndblackwatch1881.wordpress.com/2009/01/08/tommy-nutter-savile-row-strutter/ (accessed 5 May 2023).

savilerow-style.com/news/tommy-nutter-rebel-cause/ (accessed 8 May 2023).

en.wikipedia.org/wiki/Tommy_Nutter (accessed 8 May 2023).

www.stevestrange.org/blitzclub.php (accessed 16 May 2023).

en.wikipedia.org/wiki/Ashes_to_Ashes_(David_Bowie_song) (accessed 16 May 2023).

bbc.fandom.com/wiki/Top_of_the_Pops#:~:text=Originally%20broadcast%20weekly%20between%201,on%20BBC%20Two%20in%202005 (accessed 16 May 2023).

www.shutterstock.com/editorial/image-editorial/embassy-club-last-night-closing-party-london-britain-109033b (accessed 16 May 2023).

twitter.com/FlipVintage/status/1282679459280191488 (accessed 16 May 2023).

en.wikipedia.org/wiki/Tom_Gilbey_(designer) (accessed 17 May 2023).

kilburnwesthampstead.blogspot.com/2020/09/the-nutters-from-kilburn-to-beatles-and.html (accessed 17 May 2023).

www.businessoffashion.com/community/people/joan-burstein (accessed 17 May 2023).

Chapter 3

www.youtube.com/watch?v=qpBsjkAwv3A (accessed 17 May 2023).

www.royalwarrant.org/company/johns-pegg (accessed 17 May 2023).

www.thetimes.co.uk/article/ole-peder-bertelsen-obituary-kv2j0fb70 (accessed 17 May 2023).

en.wikipedia.org/wiki/John_Michael_Ingram (accessed 17 May 2023).

www.permanentstyle.com/2021/01/john-simons-the-shop-the-history-the-influence.html (accessed 17 May 2023).

www.brownsfashion.com/uk/history (accessed 17 May 2023).

www.theindustry.fashion/reviving-londons-former-streets-of-cool/ (accessed 17 May 2023).

www.per-spex.com/articles/2019/3/17/the-importance-of-the-1980s-power-suit (accessed 18 May 2023).

www.newyorker.com/magazine/1998/04/27/bad-boy-in-the-kitchen (accessed 18 May 2023).

en.wikipedia.org/wiki/Angels_Costumes#cite_note-3 (accessed 18 May 2023).

angels.uk.com/history (accessed 18 May 2023).

en.wikipedia.org/wiki/Master_cylinder (accessed 12 June 2023).

www.carthrottle.com/post/how-master-cylinders-and-slave-cylinders-work-and-their-importance/ (accessed 12 June 2023).

Chapter 4

www.bondsuits.com/the-tailor-of-panama-another-mi6-agent/ (accessed 18 May 2023).

www.reddit.com/r/askcarguys/comments/4xqf5j/how_do_i_properly_3_point_turn_use_clutch_control/ (accessed 12 June 2023).

Chapter 5

www.thetimes.co.uk/article/scott-crolla-obituary-36kmxkk98 (accessed
    18 May 2023).
www.trumanbrewery.com/cgi-bin/venue2.pl (accessed 19 May 2023).
www.motonetworks.com/christine-one-greatest-car-movies-time/ (accessed
    12 June 2023).

Chapter 6

en.wikipedia.org/wiki/Hussein_Chalayan (accessed 20 May 2023).
www.theguardian.com/uk/2004/may/27/thebritartfire.arts1 (accessed
    20 May 2023).
en.wikipedia.org/wiki/Tracey_Emin (accessed 20 May 2023).
oldspitalfieldsmarket.com/journal/a-swift-half-at-the-golden-heart (accessed
    21 May 2023).
www.tripadvisor.co.uk/Attraction_Review-g186338-d6518529-Reviews-The_
    Golden_Heart_Public_House-London_England.html (accessed 21 May 2023).
en.wikipedia.org/wiki/Mark_Powell_(clothing_designer) (accessed 21 May 2023).
www.instagram.com/p/CEtQ8g3g1p1/ (accessed 21 May 2023).
debrouxautomotive.com/is-classic-car-restoration-a-good-
    investment/#:~:text=If%20you%20plan%20to%20restore,you%20spent%20
    to%20restore%20it (accessed 12 June 2023).
www.holtsauto.com/simoniz/news/classic-car-restoration-tips-and-advice-for-
    beginners/ (accessed 12 June 2023).

Chapter 7

cxainc.com/artist/david-bradshaw/ (accessed 1 March 2023).
en.wikipedia.org/wiki/Scream_(Michael_Jackson_and_Janet_Jackson_song)
    (accessed 1 March 2023).
en.wikipedia.org/wiki/Theme_from_Mission:_Impossible (accessed 1 March 2023).
auto.howstuffworks.com/cruise-control.htm (accessed 12 June 2023).

Chapter 9

en.wikipedia.org/wiki/Dylan_Jones (accessed 21 May 2023).
www.theguardian.com/fashion/2023/apr/07/michael-roberts-obituary (accessed
    22 May 2023).

www.instagram.com/p/B6ktPsApdqO/ (accessed 22 May 2023).
www.nh-design.co.uk/nicky-haslams-biography/ (accessed 22 May 2023).
www.vogue.co.uk/arts-and-lifestyle/article/paul-smith-prized-possessions
    (accessed 22 May 2023).
www.stuartslondon.com/blog/2011/07/17/brutus-by-name/ (accessed
    22 May 2023).
www.youtube.com/watch?v=Eb3CwvPVC8I (accessed 22 May 2023).
whatfrankislisteningto.negstar.com/pop-rock/david-dundas-jeans-on-
    crysalis-1977-2/ (accessed 22 May 2023).
www.hotcars.com/why-gearheads-should-own-british-sports-car/ (accessed
    14 June 2023).
en.wikipedia.org/wiki/Team_orders (accessed 14 June 2023).

Chapter 10

www.thebeigelshop.com/about (accessed 23 May 2023).
retaildesignblog.net/2013/06/26/strasburgo-concept-store-tokyo/ (accessed
    23 May 2023).
katharinehamnett.com/gbp/biography (accessed 23 May 2023).
cp.mistore.jp/global/en/history.html (accessed 23 May 2023).
en.wikipedia.org/wiki/Patrick_Cox (accessed 24 May 2023).
www.realestate-tokyo.com/living-in-tokyo/japanese-culture/whats-tatami/
    (accessed 24 May 2023).
thefaceandid.com/collections/the-face-magazine-1995 (accessed 25 May 2023).
www.sankyoseiko.co.jp/en/company/history/ (accessed 25 May 2023).

Chapter 11

en.wikipedia.org/wiki/Apple_Corps (accessed 8 May 2023).

Chapter 12

www.dewhirst.com/what-we-do/ (accessed 27 December 2022).
www.ft.com/content/01154adc-b512-11e5-8358-9a82b43f6b2f (accessed
    27 January 2023).
www.fruitnet.com/fresh-produce-journal/marc-bolland-named-new-mands-
    ceo/150067.article#:~:text=Bolland%20will%20succeed%20current%20
    executive,breach%20of%20corporate%20best%20practice (accessed
    27 January 2023).

www.theguardian.com/fashion/2018/jun/05/why-the-man-behind-max-mara-is-the-most-influential-fashion-designer-youve-never-heard-of (accessed 26 May 2023).

aeworld.com/fashion/ian-griffiths-creative-director-at-max-mara-discusses-the-fall-winter-2022-collection/ (accessed 26 May 2023).

www.youtube.com/watch?v=3UizjqXZOqE (accessed 1 February 2023).

www.campaignlive.co.uk/article/asda-brings-back-pocket-tap-meta-ad-campaign/1693303 (accessed 6 February 2023).

books.google.co.uk/books?id=_9MJbemHOmYC&pg=PA361&lpg=PA361&dq=waterfall+australian+olympics+opening+ceremony&source=bl&ots=1Kro7aG9JZ&sig=ACfU3U0l1ZJSNz1klk6aeMtJFe4y4MdDwA&hl=en&sa=X&ved=2ahUKEwiSl67YnoX9AhXRTsAKHUGGDbEQ6AF6BAgUEAM#v=onepage&q=waterfall%20australian%20olympics%20opening%20ceremony&f=false (accessed 8 February 2023).

www.nma.gov.au/defining-moments/resources/cathy-freeman#:~:text=Cathy%20Freeman%20was%20the%20final,up%20several%20flights%20of%20stairs (accessed 8 February 2023).

www.theguardian.com/media/2010/may/19/marks-spencer-1966-world-cup (accessed 8 February 2023).

www.theguardian.com/football/2010/mar/15/david-beckham-world-cup-injury (accessed 8 February 2023).

en.wikipedia.org/wiki/Helmut_Lang_(artist) (accessed 27 May 2023).

www.adbrands.net/archive/uk/debenhams-uk-p.htm (accessed 27 May 2023).

www.thetimes.co.uk/article/my-hols-8ln6crsqjdv (accessed 27 May 2023).

www.youtube.com/watch?v=U6hFvOwV9yk (accessed 27 May 2023).

Chapter 13

rvm.pm/burt-bacharach-et-al-perform-at-the-72nd-oscars-2000/ (accessed 11 February 2023).

www.smoothradio.com/news/music/burt-bacharach-facts-age-songs-wife-children/ (accessed 12 February 2023).

www.dailymail.co.uk/news/article-11733827/Inside-Burt-Bacharachs-idyllic-Hollywood-Pacific-Palisades-homes.html (accessed 12 February 2023).

books.google.co.uk/books?id=qIj5TpxXffoC&pg=PA129&lpg=PA129&dq=burt+bacharach+2000+oscars+don+was&source=bl&ots=5WE4Ltw0MM&sig=ACfU3U33MaSZCe_inxTwIJUQMal4ZbmhjQ&hl=en&sa=X&ved=2ahUKEwi1o8-25o_9AhUdTEEAHaCUC6UQ6AF6BAg1EAM#v=onepage&q=burt%20bacharach%202000%20oscars%20don%20was&f=false (accessed 12 February 2023).

www.ft.com/content/f292b35e-a058-11e6-891e-abe238dee8e2 (accessed
    12 February 2023).
www.houseandgarden.co.uk/gallery/walk-in-wardrobe-ideas (accessed
    12 February 2023).
www.dailymail.co.uk/news/article-3599057/Family-L-Wren-Scott-reveal-sadness-
    two-year-rift-Mick-Jagger-tell-rude-Stones-frontman-never-called-girlfriend.
    html (accessed 12 February 2023).
www.smoothradio.com/news/music/best-oscars-performances-video/ (accessed
    12 February 2023).
www.chicagotribune.com/news/ct-xpm-1985-06-02-8502040727-story.html
    (accessed 16 February 2023).
www.architecturaldigest.com/gallery/ernest-hemingways-favorite-bars-around-
    world#:~:text=The%20Ritz%20(Paris%2C%20France),51%20dry%20
    martinis%20shortly%20after (accessed 16 February 2023).
www.theguardian.com/film/2012/jul/15/richard-zanuck (accessed
    16 February 2023).
www.airport-data.com/aircraft/photo/000119333.html (accessed 20 February 2023).
www.ultimateaerobatics.co.uk/training (accessed 20 February 2023).
www.laweekly.com/the-shrine-used-to-host-the-oscars-now-it-hosts-steve-aoki-
    parties/ (accessed 23 February 2023).
www.vanityfair.com/style/photos/2020/02/2000-oscars-red-carpet (accessed
    23 February 2023).
www.youtube.com/watch?v=zct1tPK1Zk0 (accessed 23 February 2023).
www.pinterest.co.uk/pin/249949848048568827/ (accessed 23 February 2023).
www.instyle.com/news/angelina-jolie-oscars-2000-brother (accessed
    23 February 2023).
www.youtube.com/watch?v=EPWpHWr1L7s (accessed 23 February 2023).
www.thephotogallery.se/faye-dunaway (accessed 23 February 2023).

Chapter 14

www.keikari.com/english/a-history-of-the-daks-waistband/ (accessed
    19 December 2022).
en.wikipedia.org/wiki/DAKS (accessed 19 December 2022).
www.drapersonline.com/news/obituary-jeremy-franks-former-chief-executive-
    daks-simpson-group (accessed 19 December 2022).
www.vogue.co.uk/article/stephen-quinn-british-vogue-publisher-to-retire
    (accessed 21 December 2022).
www.mylearning.org/stories/mands-penny-bazaars/562? (accessed
    27 December 2022).

www.drapersonline.com/news/timothy-everest-to-launch-tailored-casualwear
(accessed 23 April 2023).

Chapter 15

www.news.com.au/entertainment/celebrity-life/hook-ups-break-ups/
david-beckham-has-one-very-bright-regret-about-his-1999-wedding-to-victoria/
news-story/c4738791e7e742a4deb76ed30a9cb6bb (accessed 17 January 2023).
www.gq-magazine.co.uk/cars/article/david-beckham-cars-goodwood-2022
(accessed 14 June 2023).

Chapter 16

en.wikipedia.org/wiki/Ann_Roth (accessed 6 March 2023).
en.wikipedia.org/wiki/Moxon_Huddersfield (accessed 11 April 2023).
www.distractify.com/p/ralph-fiennes-relationship-history (accessed 20 April 2023).
www.bondsuits.com/gareth-mallory-grey-suit-trousers-braces/ (accessed
20 April 2023).
en.wikipedia.org/wiki/Prometheus_(2012_film) (accessed 22 April 2023).
en.wikipedia.org/wiki/Patrick_Grant_(designer) (accessed 29 May 2023).
www.imdb.com/title/tt0113189/characters/nm0005155 (accessed 14 June 2023).

Chapter 18

bj105.com/landmark-buildings/the-booby-trap-winter-park-defunct/ (accessed
12 February 2023).
www.forbes.com/sites/korihale/2019/11/24/jay-zs-roc-nation-gets-iconix-lawsuit-
dismissed-for-15m/?sh=12740cf96e29 (accessed 13 February 2023).
en.wikipedia.org/wiki/Rocawear (accessed 13 February 2023).
www.iconixbrand.com/about/ (accessed 13 February 2023).
en.wikipedia.org/wiki/The_Woodsman_(2004_film) (accessed 13 February 2023).
www.hiddenrsrch.com/p/heart-of-the-city (accessed 13 February 2023).
nymag.com/news/profiles/17268/ (accessed 13 February 2023).
www.carsurvey.org/reviews/maybach/57/r72458/comments/page-2/ (accessed
31 May 2023).
en.wikipedia.org/wiki/Maybach_57_and_62 (accessed 14 June 2023).

Chapter 19

www.topendsports.com/sport/list/motocross.htm (accessed 12 March 2023).

tinkadventures.com/2014/02/26/the-ridgeway-and-avebury-stone-circles/#:~:text=For%20those%20of%20you%20like,at%20Ivinghoe%20Beacon%20in%20Buckinghamshire (accessed 15 March 2023).

en.wikipedia.org/wiki/Rapha_(sportswear)#:~:text=The%20company%20was%20started%20in,ap%C3%A9ritif%20drink%20company%20Saint%20Rapha%C3%ABl (accessed 16 March 2023).

cyclinguphill.com/leith-hill-climb/ (accessed 14 June 2023).

Chapter 20

en.wikipedia.org/wiki/Order_of_the_British_Empire (accessed 30 April 2023).

www.standard.co.uk/news/london/final-plea-to-save-west-end-brutalist-treasure-car-park-from-demolition-by-hotel-giant-a4054991.html (accessed 30 April 2023).

www.iwm.org.uk/history/what-the-royal-family-did-during-the-second-world-war (accessed 2 May 2023).

www.pinterest.co.uk/pin/474566879456701431/ (accessed 2 May 2023).

en.wikipedia.org/wiki/Chancellorship_of_Gordon_Brown (accessed 2 May 2023).

www.theguardian.com/politics/shortcuts/2017/jan/27/william-hague-after-dinner-superstar-david-beckham (accessed 2 May 2023).

www.theguardian.com/uk/2009/dec/31/new-years-honours-status-quo (accessed 3 May 2023).

www.youtube.com/watch?v=vYfNL3nEww0 (accessed 3 May 2023).

www.google.com/search?q=jenson+button+honoured++mbe+&tbm=isch&ved=2ahU KEwjtudvh7Nj-AhWHmicCHe3iAe8Q2-cCegQIABAA&oq=jenson+button+ho noured++mbe+&gs_lcp=CgNpbWcQAzoECCMQJ1DnBFjSEWC-E2gBcAB4AI-ABOogBxAKSAQE2mAEAoAEBqgELZ3dzLXdpei1pbWfAAQE&sclient=im g&ei=PCtSZO2rCoe1nsEP7cWH-A4&bih=579&biw=1180&rlz=1C5CHFA_ enGB769GB769#imgrc=vY3Fr2_OIbc3WM (accessed 3 May 2023).

www.royal.uk/behind-the-scenes-investitures (accessed 3 May 2023).

glassofbubbly.com/the-history-of-champagne-in-sports-wins/ (accessed 14 June 2023).

Chapter 21

www.labelnetworks.com/bread-butter-back-in-berlin-launches-a-successful-show-for-street-urban-and-denim-brands-in-the-historic-berlin-tempelhof-airport/ (accessed 19 January 2023).

www.brooksengland.com/en_uk/ (accessed 24 January 2023).

en.wikipedia.org/wiki/Boxpark (accessed 24 January 2023).

www.extrauk.co.uk/brooks/about-brand (accessed 24 January 2023).

www.drapersonline.com/companies/multiples-and-etailers/austin-reed-sells-regent-street-flagship-to-supergroup (accessed 24 January 2023).

www.telegraph.co.uk/finance/newsbysector/retailandconsumer/8536516/Superdry-in-12m-Austin-Reed-deal.html (accessed 24 January 2023).

en.wikipedia.org/wiki/Performance_(film) (accessed 24 January 2023).

en.wikipedia.org/wiki/Our_Man_Flint (accessed 25 January 2023).

www.britishfashioncouncil.co.uk/event/1279/London-Collections-Men-SS17 (accessed 26 January 2023).

www.theguardian.com/business/1999/nov/07/observerbusiness.marksspencer (accessed 27 January 2023).

travel.nine.com.au/destinations/sex-and-the-city-locations/c8c4d313-6b4b-474f-b273-b2e690eead0f#9 (accessed 27 January 2023).

www.youtube.com/watch?v=B49OYx1uJww (accessed 8 June 2023).

www.theguardian.com/technology/2015/apr/26/morgan-three-wheeler-car-review-martin-love (accessed 14 June 2023).

Chapter 22

en.wikipedia.org/wiki/AllSaints (accessed 24 April 2023).

rules.co.uk/wp-content/uploads/2013/11/Rules-Drink-Menu.pdf (accessed 26 April 2023).

www.bournemouthecho.co.uk/news/23386285.car-falls-huge-sinkhole-appears-suddenly-poole/ (accessed 14 June 2023).

Chapter 23

www.greyflannel.co.uk/blogs/major-flannels-journal/major-flannel-presents-founder-owners-in-conversation (accessed 29 April 2023).

graziadaily.co.uk/beauty-hair/wellness/chiltern-firehouse-hottest-restaurant-town/ (accessed 29 April 2023).

www.monclondon.com/blogs/monc-journey/an-insider-s-guide-chiltern-st-marylebone (accessed 29 April 2023).

en.wikipedia.org/wiki/Chiltern_Firehouse (accessed 29 April 2023).

Index

You may also enjoy ...

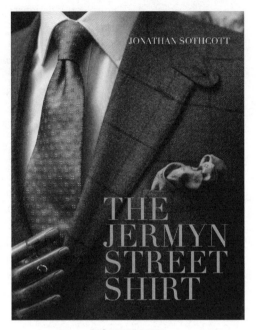

978 0 7509 9417 0

A wealth of sartorial showbusiness anecdotes as well as style tips from some of the big screen's most dapper stars. With unique access to many of the makers, including Turnbull & Asser, Hilditch & Key and Budd, Jonathan Sothcott presents an expertly curated pictorial treasure trove of previously unseen ephemera, including celebrity shirt patterns and samples.

The History Press

The destination for history
www.thehistorypress.co.uk